scm centrebooks

Christianity at the Centre / John Hic
Who is God? / D. W. D. Shaw
What about the Old Testament? / J
What is the New Testament? / T. G. A. Baker
What is the Church? / Victor de Waal
What is Right? / Michael Keeling
The Last Things Now / David L. Edwards
Who is Jesus Christ? / A. O. Dyson

David L Edwards

The Last Things Now

SCM PRESS LTD

334 00878 6

First published 1969
by SCM Press Ltd
56 Bloomsbury Street London WC1

© *SCM Press Ltd 1969*

Printed in Great Britain by
Billing & Sons Limited
Guildford and London

To Helen,
Katharine and Clare,
before they need to think
about these things

Contents

Preface

The 'last things' are traditionally pictured as death, judgment, heaven and hell. In the twentieth century they may seem to have become evolution, progress, disaster and extinction. When the Editor of the SCM Press challenged me to write a short book about these things I could scarcely refuse, despite the difficulties involved. It is a fair question to address to any Christian teacher, what a modern man may rightly be expected to believe about his destiny. Besides, I remembered how when I held the Editor's job it fell to me to publish a good deal of technical writing about 'biblical eschatology' and some philosophical discussions about the ideas of God and the soul, but it was more difficult to find an author who was willing to try to write more simply while taking the scholarly discussion into account. I hoped, therefore, that if I made an attempt some non-experts might be interested, and one or two of the experts might be glad of the opportunity to say why this kind of presentation will not do. I was strengthened in my hope by invitations to deliver in Norwich Cathedral, at St Augustine's College, Canterbury, and at a course arranged by the Central Readers' Board of the Church of England, lectures on which this book is based.

I have quoted the Bible freely. Quotations from the Old Testament are usually given in the Revised Standard Version, and New Testament quotations in the translation of the New English Bible.

I am greatly indebted to the Dean of York and to three senior colleagues in the Faculty of Divinity at Cambridge, Professor Moule, Professor Nineham and Dr Norman Pittenger, for their comments on these pages.

King's College, Cambridge   D.L.E.

1 Thoughts before Dying

1 Death Comes to the Modern World

Death seems to have replaced sex as the great unmentionable, and the nervousness of the few magazine articles which break the silence only goes to prove it. Respectable people used to cover themselves heavily while swimming and always avoided rude references to reproduction. Now everyone enjoys undressing, the railway bookstalls show that few young women have any clothes left, and supper parties argue freely about contraception and homosexuality. However, we prefer to bury the idea of death, in strong contrast with the fuss which used to be made over death-bed farewells, viewing the corpse, the funeral procession, the service around the grave, mourning, monuments and all the rest of the mortal pageant.

Nowadays dying people are expected to join the general conspiracy that they will get better. Indeed, they *do* live longer than any previous generation expected, and they die more easily, thanks to modern medicine. Deathbeds are somehow not fashionable. When death has come, the survivors are not expected to grieve more than a little – and that little must be in private. A tendency is growing for people to avoid both the dying and the mourners, out of sheer embarrassment.

Why, then, write a book about death? For one very good reason. Although the subject can now be approached a little more calmly, deep down people are still interested. In the poorer countries, death remains a near neighbour. In the richer countries, the road accidents have not been the only human sacrifices to modern progress. The two world wars not only resulted in casualties far greater than those in any previous conflict, but also killed many of those millions in circumstances as horrible as any atrocity in the past. The shooting and gassing of the best of Europe's manhood in the fight for a few square miles in 1914–18, the scientific murder of six million Jews, and the destruction of great cities by bombs are things not easily forgotten. For our century has *witnessed* these horrors (and so many lesser acts of violence), whereas previous atrocities would usually only be spoken about. When we remember that in a modern home Granny is not likely to be dying upstairs, let us not forget that death will be shown every evening on the TV set in the living room.

The recreations of rich societies may not involve animal blood, but they certainly involve a great deal of tomato ketchup. Films of the Wild West would be impossible, according to the convention, without much shooting and much dying in the dust. The hero rides to triumph along the Valley of the Shadow of Death. Crime fiction does not normally begin with an income-tax swindle or a bank robbery – a corpse must provide the climax of evil and the occasion of vengeance. In these modern forms of entertainment, ancient myths of good versus bad are dressed up anew, but still on the old basis of life versus death. Look through a list of recent book titles. 'Death' is no longer the explicit subject of many serious books, but the mention of it still seems a selling point in the titles of innumerable novels.

Serious fiction (or drama or film) in our century is very often acutely conscious of death as the final futility;[1] and death dominates many twentieth-century philosophies. The whole literature of existentialism, for example, finds 'authentic existence' by coming to terms with the end. The being of man (or 'Being-itself', if such a mystery is dealt with) is defined by contrasting it with death's Non-Being. Heidegger, Sartre and many others teach the intellectuals that their lives must always be lived in the light thrown by their coming deaths. We all die, and each one of us dies alone; death is what shows the individual that he is finite and that he is solitary. Many psychologists join the philosophers here. Sigmund Freud confessed that he thought about his death every day of his life, and the psychoanalysis which he pioneered emphasized the fascination of *Thanatos* (Death) equally with the fascination of *Eros* (Love).

Of course, we do not need to go to television or to books to know that death still makes victims of our emotions. We know people who mourn, and by helpless sympathy we know that grief is itself like a disease. The tightness in the throat, the choking, the sighing, the tears, the empty stomach, the weak muscles, the sense of guilt that one has survived, the hypocrisy of one's courage, the loss of warmth towards others, the irritation whether people sympathize (are they really gloating?) or stay away (do they care nothing?), the ache which comes when one has felt for a stupid moment that death had never taken place, at other times the difficulty of recalling how the dead looked, the living in the past, the longing to join the dead . . . some of us can look into our own experience for all this. And all of us know that a society which authorizes few outlets for the expression of grief is punishing those who mourn. No wonder that many people say that what they fear most is not death, but its consequences to those whom they love!

But which of us can in his heart say that he knows nothing of the fear of death? In a recent book written in order to attack the hope of immortality, an English agnostic has written about the consolations which philosophy can offer to mortals. 'only a small minority of exceptionally self-disciplined people can benefit from them, and even they can do so only in their better moments'.[2] The same writer quotes a modern poet:

> The tin toys of the hawker move on the pavement inch by inch
> Not knowing they are wound up. It is better to be so
> Than to be, like us, wound up and, while running down, to know.[3]

It seems, therefore, that any suggestion that people have

lost interest in death would be an exaggeration. In modern countries, we are not quite so exposed to death's perils and pains as all previous generations were. We are not quite so afraid of death in general, or of our own deaths in particular. Yet we are still deeply aware that the mortality rate is 100 per cent. 'I remain convinced,' wrote the author of another recent attack on the idea of a future life, 'that the subject of death and immortality is of the utmost importance for thinking men, and that they cannot work through to a mature philosophy of life without coming to a definite conclusion about it.'[4]

2 *Survival in Sheol*

At first sight, nothing seems more improbable than that the survivors should think that the dead person, too, has survived. The lifeless body before them grows cold, stiff, smelly and rotten unless it is destroyed by fire. Not the least flicker of a communication comes from the mind which so obviously depended on the body before the body became a corpse. The rest is silence. Nowadays some patients can be snatched back from apparent death, and nurses and undertakers may soften or conceal some of the grimmer aspects of the end, but there still comes the terrible moment when even the most brilliant of doctors must say: 'I have done all I could.' In a modern hospital we seem to be in exactly the same position which the poet who wrote the Book of Job knew some 2,300 years ago:

For there is hope for a tree,
  if it be cut down, that it will sprout again, and that its shoots will not cease . . .
But man dies, and is laid low;
  man breathes his last, and where is he? . . .
So man lies down and rises not again;
  till the heavens are no more he will not awake, or be roused out of his sleep . . .
If a man die, shall he live again?

(Job 14.7, 10, 12, 14)

An amazing fact about the history of man is that so many millions have refused to accept death as the complete

14

truth. Human bones have been discovered which were surrounded by the stone implements which primitive men then used, and which were painted with red ochre. The most probable explanation seems to be that Stone Age man believed that some kind of life remained in his dead – or pretended that he so believed.

The usual belief among relatively primitive peoples is that the dead are like the living, only weaker. Death is to be feared, regretted and lamented, but it is not extinction. It is like a very bad wound, or like a sick man's worst moments. The dead are able to watch the rituals which are performed after their own deaths. They are also able to make their presence felt if these rituals are neglected, or if the survivors behave in some other way contrary to the customs which the dead accepted when they were alive. The dead can, indeed, do much harm to the living if provoked – and, being jealous of the living, they are quite easily provoked. The double motive of primitive people's treatment of the dead is, therefore, to keep the dead happy – and to keep them away.

Although a vast modern literature describes these primitive beliefs, we have little need to go beyond the Old Testament in order to discover what the life of the dead was thought to be like. The Bible is full of passages which show how much Ancient Israel shared 'heathen' beliefs about the dead. The chapter of the Book of Job already quoted also contains a reference to 'Sheol'. Sheol was the abode of the dead in Hebrew mythology. It is mentioned, for example, in a brief and forlorn prayer to be remembered and sheltered by Yahweh (God) when dead (Job 14.13). To offer such a prayer was an act of courage, for the normal Hebrew belief was that God himself regarded death as a threat. This threat was part of the divine wrath, as in the Book of Hosea (13.14):

> Shall I ransom them from the power of Sheol?
> Shall I redeem them from Death?
> O Death, where are your plagues?
> O Sheol, where is your destruction?

Another passage in Job is very famous because it seems to suggest a hope that the dead will have the joy of seeing God:

> For I know that my avenger (*goel*) lives,
>   and at the last he will stand upon the earth,
> and after my skin has been thus destroyed,
>   then without (or in, or from) my flesh I shall see God,
> whom I shall see on my side (or for myself),
>   and my eyes shall behold, and not another.
>
> (Job 19.25–27)

This passage has been loved all the more because many translations have made the obscure Hebrew read 'in my flesh' as an anticipation of the old Christian belief in the resurrection of the body, and have made the mysterious Hebrew reference to the *goel* read like an anticipation of the divine Redeemer.[5] The old translation of another passage (Job 13.15) also presented the dying Job as a man of near-Christian faith: 'though he slay me, yet will I trust in him'.

However, the truth seems to be that the Book of Job nowhere suggests that the answer to the problem of suffering is that the dead will be happy. The best translation of the sentence just quoted seems to be: 'Behold, he will slay me; I have no hope.' The most that can be said in favour of Sheol is:

> There the wicked cease from troubling,
>   and there the weary are at rest.
> There the prisoners are at ease together;
>   they hear not the voice of the taskmaster.
> The small and the great are there,
>   and the slave is free from his master.   (Job 3.17-19)

As Job's suffering increases, so does his wish to die – but this wish is never a hope, for

> if I look for Sheol as my house,
>   if I spread my couch in darkness,
> if I say to the pit, 'You are my father',
>   and to the worm, 'You are 'My mother', or 'My sister',
> where then is my hope?
>   Who will see my hope?   (Job 17.13–15)

The passage about the *goel* may, therefore, refer not to a supernatural Redeemer, but to Job's next of kin, the ordinary *goel* or avenger responsible in Hebrew custom for the requital of wrong done to the family. Job may hope to be avenged on earth in the normal way; and his further hope may be not that he will see God 'without my flesh', eternally, but that he will see God 'from my flesh' – at the extremity of sickness, before death. The passage is ambiguous, as the variety in the translations shows, and it merely leads to a further lament, 'My heart faints within me!' (Job 19.27). The Book of Job as we have it (was there an earlier, shorter version?) makes it clear how Job's vindication *did* come: 'fourteen thousand sheep, six thousand camels, a thousand yoke of oxen, and a thousand she-asses . . . also seven sons and three daughters' (Job 42.12, 13).

The Book of Isaiah shows how depression would overwhelm a king such as Hezekiah when he feared that his sickness would be fatal. 'I am consigned to the gates of Sheol for the rest of my years. I said, I shall not see the Lord in the land of the living' (Isa. 38.10–11). When Hezekiah recovered, he made no pretence about preferring death to life, even in his prayer:

For Sheol cannot thank thee,
   death cannot praise thee;
those who go down into the pit cannot hope for thy faithfulness.
The living, the living, he thanks thee,
   as I do this day.   (Isa. 38.18–19)

And here again we cannot be surprised; for those in Sheol were known as the Rephaim (the Shades or Weaklings), and when a king of Babylon was pictured as entering Sheol, his fellow-Rephaim could gloat: 'You too have become as weak as we!' (Isa. 14.10).

'One fate comes to all,' an eloquent Jew concluded, 'to the righteous and the wicked, to the good and the evil, to the clean and the unclean, to him who sacrifices and him who does not sacrifice. . . . He who is joined with all the living has hope, for a living dog is better than a dead lion. For the living know that they will die, but the dead know nothing. . . . Their love and their hate and their envy have already perished, and they have no more for ever any share in all that is done under the sun' (Eccles. 9.2, 4–6).

So we can see in the Old Testament a fear of death which is accompanied by the further horror of the primitive belief that the dead are not completely dead. Amid the plagues of death they may 'see' God, but they cannot praise him. They may recognize a fallen king, but that is no consolation for their own state – the state in which, while half-alive, they 'know nothing'. And we can guess the origins of such beliefs. Yahweh was thought of as a sky-god. Sheol was thought of as a cave, or as a number of caves, beneath the earth. We can imagine how the more mysterious caves in Palestine frightened the Israelites (as they must have frightened primitive man while he had to take shelter in them). Some caves were used as burial places, where the dead members of a family would be laid on slabs. When a fresh corpse was 'gathered to his fathers', the mourners would see the generations of the family laid out on each side of this cave – looking and yet not looking, dead and yet alive in that darkness, alive and yet not alive. So the imagination fed on thoughts about the dead, while the reason knew with the women of Tekoa that 'we must all die, we are like water spilt on the ground, which cannot be gathered up again' (II Sam. 14.14).

Similar ideas about the dead can be found in Ancient Greece, where Hades was the equivalent of Sheol, and in many other places. Such ideas cannot fairly be described as 'religious wishful thinking' – for no one wished to join the dead, and many seem to have shared Hamlet's belief that the fear of something after death was what made suicide no escape from life's miseries. Indeed, the higher forms of religion often discouraged such ideas, because an obsession with the dead distracted people from their duties to the living and to the living God or gods. In Ancient Egypt, Pharaoh Ikhnaton tried to concentrate all worship on the sun, in opposition to the cult of the dead.

The Old Testament contains a number of warnings against attempts to get into touch with the dead. It was believed that Yahweh had informed Moses: 'If a person turns to mediums and wizards . . . I will set my face against that person' (Lev. 20.6). Accordingly all mediums should be put to death (Deut. 18.11). When Saul was a good king, he naturally carried out this divine law. When he persuaded the Witch of Endor to 'bring up' Samuel from the dead, he got what he deserved – the promise from the half-alive prophet that 'tomorrow you and your sons shall be with me' (I Sam. 28.19).

However, it is clear that, whether or not religious leaders discouraged an interest in the dead, popular religion had to cope with the challenge of death to the emotions. Those who had been dragged down by the disaster of death had some-how to be fitted into the world over which the God or gods of a particular religion ruled. So pictures such as those of the Hebrew Sheol or the Greek Hades survive, to show how the basic, primitive belief in survival after death was made part of the whole pattern of a people's religious beliefs.

3 *Survival in Spiritualism*

In the twentieth century, belief of this kind lingers on among primitive peoples and, in modern countries, among the small minorities which are interested in Spiritualism. That comparison of primitives and Spiritualists may be resented, for to call a group 'primitive' may seem an insult – and an insult to the Spiritualist movement may seem an injustice, for this group includes many sincere (and many sad) people. But the key to the comparison is the fact that both Sheol and Spiritualism stand for *the survival of the dead without any real regard to morality or to religion*. In this way of thinking, survival seems a fact of death. As the Old Testament said, it applies equally 'to him who sacrifices and to him who does not sacrifice'. But it does not lead to any ethical or religious glory. Those who believed in Sheol thought that the half-alive dead were worse off than the living. Those who believe in Spiritualism think that the dead with their ethereal bodies are better off. But essentially, the same life goes on for ever.

The history of Spiritualism – that is, of organized contact with the dead through mediums – is as large, as mysterious and on the whole as depressing as Sheol itself. Fortunately little need be said about it here. Many great cruelties have been inflicted on men and women suspected of being witches and wizards – cruelties which often found their pretext in orthodox religion. On the other hand, probably not all witches were entirely nice in the bad old days, the witchcraft which survives can be more than an eccentric romanticism, and many frauds are known to have been perpetrated by modern mediums. A great deal of attention by some scientifically minded people has been given to the history of witchcraft, to the exposure of fraudulent mediums, and to the investigation of phenomena. The Society for Psychical Research was founded in Britain in 1882, and has equivalents in other countries.

When one reads the literature of Spiritualism, one is often inclined to marvel at the incredulity of its critics. In case after case, according to the Spiritualists, human survival of bodily death has been proved because the dead have made contact with the living through a medium. One is often inclined to ask: can anything except prejudice deny that these thrilling events took place? But when one closes the propaganda of the organized Spiritualist movement, and opens instead the journals and books of the more scientific 'psychical researchers', one sees why Spiritualism failed. It looked like being a large-scale movement when people bereaved in 1914–18 wanted comfort without being able to embrace the consolations of religion, but it has not secured a widespread, lasting popularity. Most modern people will not go near the twentieth-century successors of the Witch of Endor.

For after all the investigations, it is still extremely uncertain whether the twentieth-century successors of the ghost of Samuel are, or are not, visitors to the earth from a life after death. They may be projections from the minds of the twentieth-century successors of Saul, and some strength is lent to the suggestion that they are by the fact that – unlike the grim promise at Endor – their messages seem always to be what the successors of Saul wish to hear. Of course, *some* investigators of psychical phenomena consider the Spiritualist case to be proved, just as *some* consider all mediums to be fraudulent. Most, however, prefer the verdict by which juries in Scotland can avoid a decision: 'not proven'. If they are presented with some definite phenomena, investigators who grant the sincerity both of the medium and of the person who is trying to get into touch with the dead can offer some explanations which do not include human immortality.

One explanation is that the medium can 'read' the mind of the modern Saul, by telepathy. Thus the medium can discover what Saul thinks that Samuel would be, do and say; and the medium can 'oblige', perhaps without any conscious attempt at fraud. It is now widely thought that mental communications can occur between people who do not speak or write to each other, and who cannot even see or touch each other. Probably many people – particularly married people or twins – have personal experience of this. If this is granted, it opens up fascinating prospects of future scientific study of the life of the mind. But to agree that 'telepathy' is possible is not to grant the survival of the dead.

But suppose 'telepathy' is not an adequate explanation? If it is granted that what the medium experiences really *is* Samuel, not Saul, then a further explanation can be offered. It can be said – and it often is said by scientifically minded investigators – that a person may make an impression on the atmosphere of a place, an impression which science cannot yet analyse. This impression can remain (it seems) when the person is absent. A similar impression might have been made by a person who has recently died. That may be what we experience. Here may be the basis of all ghost stories. Or it may be granted that the impression comes directly from the person who is dead. (Many people have reported experiences in which a bit of them floats in the air and looks down on the body, and this *may* suggest that a man might be able to witness his own funeral.) But it can still be said that the psychical powers of the dead person are active for only a limited time, like the fading smile on the face of the Cheshire Cat. The *psi* bit of a person may float away, and linger on for a few years – but that, too, is not immortality.

As one reads these cautious verdicts or non-verdicts by those who investigate Spiritualism, one may often wonder why they are so suspicious. The writer of the Books of Samuel seems to have felt no difficulty in introducing a ghost into his narrative, any more than Shakespeare did in *Hamlet* or *Macbeth*. He told the story, and went on without a pause. Why is the twentieth century so much more nervous about admitting the existence of these spirits?

The answer seems to be that a great change has taken place in our attitude to the dead, under the pressure of civilization and of civilization's proudest achievement: the scientific method. The attitude of most civilized people today is that death, whatever else it does, makes the greatest difference imaginable to a person. It is not convincing to say that a dead person is weaker, half-alive or ethereal. A *dead* person must be completely, or almost completely, *different*. And it is not enough to think that the dead person takes only an occasional interest in the things of this life, or is interested in these things in an ineffective or jealous way. The dead person has been removed by death from the whole sphere of the life which we know.

In Spiritualism, the fatal weakness does not lie in the fraudulent practices of many mediums or in the cynicism of the organizers who trade by feeding grief. Some of the agents and sponsors of others movements – religious, political, artistic or scientific – are open to some similar criticisms, and wise students of human nature have to decide whether, despite all these moral defects, there is 'anything in' religion, politics, art or science. The fatal weakness of Spiritualism, to the mind of the twentieth century, lies in the usual triviality of its messages. Almost all of the so-called 'messages from the dead' consist of little bits of information about life on earth, or little bits of encouraging news to the effect that the after-life is like the pleasanter parts of life on earth. Heaven is presented as a celestial holiday camp. This offends the whole modern sense of the gravity of death. If the dead are really alive, we feel that they should have entered a life infinitely superior to our little days; and because the messages are so trivial, our conclusion tends to be that they originate in the minds of the people who are interested in Spiritualism.

It is no answer to our objection to say (as the more sensitive Spiritualists often do) that these messages would be nobler if the mediums were nobler. We must judge the messages which are offered to us. Nor is it an answer to say that some experiences which are believed to have involved communication with the dead have been of a far higher quality, spiritually, ethically and intellectually, or to have been a wordless, ineffable reassurance. Such experiences do occur. But a humble, grateful wonder after such experiences is not what keeps the Spiritualist movement in business.

Previous generations might have found little difficulty in accepting the Spiritualists' messages from the half-alive dead – from a literary genius who had now forgotten his basic grammar, or from a profoundly sensitive lover who now could speak to his beloved no more than a few words as in a telegram. But, rather than imagine the dead in an immortal or semi-immortal half-life, our generation is one which hears the consoling words spoken by the philosopher Epicurus about 300 years before Christ: 'While we are here, death is not, and when death is here, we are not.' 'Death,' said the twentieth-century philosopher Wittgenstein, 'is not an event in life. Death is not lived through. . . . The world in death does not change, but ceases.'[6]

4 *The Resurrection of the Body*

There may be an alternative to extinction at death. At

least, many millions of people have thought so, believing that
death may be the gate to a fuller, better life. *Death or glory!*
This alternative may be put in words which have become
immortal (or the next best thing) from the speech of
Socrates to the judges who had condemned him to death,
at the end of Plato's *Apology*:

> There is great reason to hope that death is good; for one of
> two things – either death is a state of nothingness and utter un-
> consciousness, or, as men say, there is a change and migration of the
> soul from this world to another. Now if you suppose that there
> is no consciousness, but a sleep like the sleep of him who is un-
> disturbed even by dreams, death will be an unspeakable gain. . . .
> But if death is the journey to another place, and there, as men say,
> all the dead abide, what good, O my friends and judges, can be
> greater than this? . . . The hour of departure has arrived, and we
> go our ways – I to die, and you to live. Which is better God only
> knows.

Many have believed that the manner of a person's
survival is related to his spiritual condition. If that condition is good, he may enter a deathless glory. The one
problem to be solved is how this can be managed; and
again we can turn to the Old Testament, to see how men
have wrestled with this problem.

The psalms contain a number of passages which can be
used in this connection, but their original meaning was
probably *not* a belief in glory after death. The most famous
of all the psalms, 23 ('The Lord is my shepherd'), originally
offered thanks for deliverance from misery (the 'valley of
deep darkness' in verse 4), and thanks for the joy of worship
all the days of the worshipper's life. It was like another
psalm of deliverance:

> Therefore my heart is glad, and my soul rejoices;
>   my body also dwells secure.
> For thou dost not give me up to Sheol,
>   or let thy godly one see the Pit. (Ps. 16.9, 10)

Other phrases which have been applied to a glory after
death referred originally (it is now thought by many
scholars) to the good life of praising Yahweh morning by

morning. (Examples include Ps. 17.15; 49.15; 73.24, 26.) No clear hope of a lasting deliverance from Sheol was possible in the psalms, although such a hope could have its origin in a psalmist's faith that the God who was his 'portion' would be with him for ever:

> Whither shall I go from thy Spirit?
> Or whither shall I flee from thy presence?
> If I ascend to heaven, thou art there!
> If I make my bed in Sheol, thou art there!   (Ps. 139.7, 8)

Another belief in Israel was that a few, specially favoured, might even escape the pains of dying. A chariot and horses of fire had descended from heaven for Elijah (II Kings 2.11), and a similar legend about Enoch was built on the verse, 'Enoch walked with God; and he was not, for God took him' (Gen. 5.24; see Heb. 11.5). A much later – not biblical – legend that the Virgin Mary was 'assumed' into heaven without dying, which was decreed by Pope Pius XII in 1950 as a compulsory dogma, may be compared with these stories.

When a lasting deliverance from Sheol was prophesied in the Old Testament, it was in the crude shape of *the resurrection or revival of a corpse*. The earliest surviving reference to this hope may come in the course of a psalm of unknown authorship and date which has been incorporated into the Book of Isaiah. 'Other lords besides thee' who have ruled over Israel will remain 'shades' – meaning 'they are dead, they will not live' (Isa. 26.14). But Israel's own dead will enjoy a better end:

> Thy dead shall live, their bodies shall rise.
> O dwellers in the dust, awake and sing for joy!
> For thy dew is a dew of light,
> and on the land of the shades thou wilt let it fall.
>
> (Isa. 26.19)

So the heavenly light would dawn on Sheol, and the select few would be restored to the good life in the only way in which the Hebrews could imagine it: 'their bodies shall rise'. But what exactly does this prophecy mean? It may mean what believers in a resurrection to an eternal glory would like it to mean. Certainly, in the Book of Isaiah as we have it, this psalm is placed immediately after a prophecy about a feast which is to be held 'for all peoples' on Mount Zion, a prophecy which includes the great verse: 'He will swallow up death for ever, and the Lord God will wipe away tears from all faces, and the reproach of his people he will take away from all the earth' (Isa. 25.8). But that prophecy's reference to the end of 'death' and 'the reproach' is itself not entirely clear, and this psalm may have been intended to refer in a poetic way to a better future for the nation Israel – just as Ezekiel's vision of the dry bones coming together and being clothed with flesh was a poetic way of saying that independence would be restored to the nation after its exile in Babylon (Ezek. 37).

The only clear reference to a *post mortem* glory in the whole of the Old Testament is, in fact, a single reference in the Book of Daniel. This was written between 168 and 165 BC. Its purpose was to strengthen the courage of Jews resisting Antiochus IV Epiphanes. This king had desecrated Yahweh's temple at Jerusalem, and was trying to stamp out the sterner elements in Judaism in order that Palestine might fit more smoothly into the Greek culture around the Eastern Mediterranean. A rebellion in defence of the old religion of Yahweh was being led by the heroic Maccabees. This rebellion had already cost lives. Were these martyrs for Judaism to have no more hope of glory? Indeed, were all the many heroes of Israel's history doomed to the shadowy half-life of Sheol? And were those who had tortured and killed these martyrs to escape punishment? The author of the Book of Daniel had a more encouraging future to offer his fellow-members of the Resistance, and a threat worse than Sheol to offer their enemies. So came the great sentence. 'And many of those who sleep in the dust of the earth shall awake, some to everlasting life, some to shame and everlasting contempt' (Dan. 12.2).

At the time this promise won a propaganda victory, as may be seen from the story of the Maccabean revolt (specially II Macc. 7 in the Apocrypha of the Old Testament,

26

the story of a mother and her seven sons who were tortured to death rather than eat pork). Many 'were tortured to death, disdaining release, to win a better resurrection', as the New Testament recalled (Heb. 11.35). But as an alternative to sleep in the dust of the earth, this kind of resurrection has not seemed plausible to mankind. The heart of this stupendous miracle was to be the revival of bodies which had suffered unjustly ('they were stoned, they were sawn in two, they were put to the sword', Heb. 11.37). All the processes of the universe were to be interrupted in order to pay honour to these Jewish heroes, and in order to satisfy their desire to see their oppressors humiliated.

Such a strange hope could be formed only in a situation of great emotional intensity, when despair, defiance and hatred crushed all everyday considerations; and it could be inspired only by a strange genius or the leader of a spiritual movement. It becomes a little easier to understand if we discover who that genius was. The author of the Book of Daniel was an intense visionary, but not a genius. He seems to have taken the idea, however indirectly, from the Persian prophet Zoroaster.

In or about 588 BC this prophet began to denounce the religion of Persia. He was forced to flee to a neighbouring country, where his message established itself. It was a message of striking originality, which included vivid promises of immortality for the good ('the followers of Truth', i e. Zoroaster's teaching) and everlasting torment for the wicked ('the followers of the Lie', i.e. the Persian religion). Zoroaster's followers added a promise that at the end of the world a Saviour (*Saoshyant*) would appear, descended from Zoroaster but born miraculously. This Saviour would raise the bodies of the dead. In developed Zoroastrianism, all these bodies, of good and wicked alike, were to be plunged into a sea of molten lead, were to emerge purified, and were to enter Paradise. This last promise to the wicked would not appeal to the Maccabean rebels for whom the Book of Daniel was written, but many scholars believe that the influence of this Persian creed on the Jews was considerable. Many Jews had contacts with Persia, or lived there; above all, the emotional situation of the Jews came to resemble the emotional situation of the Zoroastrian.

Devout Jews, like the Zoroastrians, begin to see life in terms of an epic struggle between the Truth and Lie, with good and wicked Spirits fighting invisibly above the earthly struggle. That picture is found in the Book of Daniel, in the Dead Sea Scrolls, and elsewhere in the evidence about Judaism in the last period before Christ. But that whole picture has faded as the conflict which produced it has been buried in history. There are just over 100,000 followers of Zoroaster left in the world today (the Parsee community in India). The Maccabean rebels, the Dead Sea Scrolls community and the Jews who fought against Rome to the end have slept in the dust for about two thousand years.

Judaism has itself almost entirely abandoned the fantasy of a physical resurrection. Many rabbis have taken the words about the 'many' awakening out of their original context, and have made them refer to the resurrection of mankind as a whole. Many rabbis, at least in modern times, have also understood the physical nature of the awakening as being no more than a symbol for an eternal life which will really be entirely spiritual. Maimonides, the greatest Jewish theologian, who lived AD 1135–1204, taught that the resurrection bodies would also perish after a time, and only the souls of the righteous would be immortal.

5 The Immortality of the Soul

Although Maimonides stated that belief in a physical resurrection was universal among his fellow-Jews in the Middle Ages, a more spiritual hope had been preserved in the Apocrypha of the Old Testament. There *The Wisdom of Solomon*, which was probably written in Alexandria less than fifty years before Christ, declared that

> God created man for incorruption,
> and made him an image of his own eternity. (Wisd. 2.23)

This 'incorruption' was seen to involve both rewards for the righteous and punishments for the wicked in Sheol:

> The souls of the righteous are in the hand of God,
>   and no torment will ever touch them.
> In the eyes of the foolish they seemed to have died,
>   and their departure was thought to be an affliction,
>   and their going from us to be their destruction;
>   but they are at peace.
> For though in the sight of men they were punished,
>   their hope is full of immortality.   (Wisd. 3.1–4)

We must note also that, mixed with this belief in the immortality of souls, there remained a more characteristically Jewish belief in a more physical and political reward to come, expressed in these words:

> In the time of their visitation they will shine forth,
>   and will run like sparks through the stubble.
> They will govern nations and rule over peoples,
>   and the Lord will reign over them for ever.   (Wisd. 3.7-8)

But who *are* these 'souls' who will not be touched by any torment after death? The Greek thought which influenced that passage in *The Wisdom of Solomon* promised immortality not to the 'righteous' who worshipped Yahweh but to the 'wise' – a category which might be as narrow as some professional philosophers with their brighter pupils. The message of Plato (who died about 347 BC), of the Neo-Platonist philosophers and of the Orphic teachers before them was that the souls of the 'wise' escaped death and entered glory because these souls were easily detachable from the bodies. The slogan of Neo-Platonism was that the body (*soma*) was a tomb (*sema*). The body could be left to its destruction, and the soul would be far better off without it. A number of arguments could be produced by Platonists to prove that, even during this life, the soul was already known to exist independently of the body. Indeed, it was argued that the soul had existed before the birth of the body, and some evidence was produced: children were thought to remember the glory from which they had come, a charming fantasy which was immortalized for all lovers of English poetry by William Wordsworth's *Ode on Intimations of Immortality from Recollections of Early Childhood.*

> Our birth is but a sleep and a forgetting:
> The Soul that rises with us, our life's Star,
> Hath had elsewhere its setting,
>   And cometh from afar:
>   Not in entire forgetfulness,
>   And not in utter nakedness,
> But trailing clouds of glory do we come
>   From God, who is our home:
> Heaven lies about us in our infancy!

However, such Platonic arguments about continuing souls have fared no better than the Jewish hopes of awakening and arising bodies. If some philosophers have felt that their mental powers needed no support from their bodies, their competitors have been willing enough to argue otherwise. (Aristotle, for example, taught that the soul was the 'form' of the body.) In no case is a philosopher known to have gone on philosophizing after getting rid of his bodily 'tomb'. The great beauty of Socrates' farewell to his disciples, as reconstructed in Plato's *Phaedo*, has not blinded men to the possibility that when the hemlock had done its work the mind of Socrates existed only in its influence on the disciples – that Socrates was, after all, mortal.

Indeed, the common man has, on the whole, not cared very much for this appeal to the superiority of the wise man's soul. Why should philosophy provide the passport to immortality? If Homer's heroes do not in fact carry on feasting in the Elysian fields to which they looked forward, why should the philosophers of Greece carry on thinking? If there is no Valhalla for the Vikings at the end of the last voyage, and no Happy Hunting Ground for the Red Indians, why should there be a timeless Academy in an immaterial Realm of Ideas?

This whole Platonic doctrine of the immortality of the soul was, of course, conceived as the most sublime compliment imaginable to the intellectual powers which the Greeks experienced and exercised in intoxicating achievements of the mind. But the average man, with his feet on the ground, has probably always failed to share the ancient philosophical belief that the 'mind' or the 'soul' could be separated from the body like a hat; and in recent years almost all philosophers have come round to a less intellectual view of life, renouncing the magic of Plato's rhetoric and abandoning the various philosophies which are covered by the technical term 'idealism'. The mind is no longer regarded as a ghost in the machine of the body, and the soul is no longer pictured as an angel temporarily imprisoned in a tomb. The word 'mind', if it is used at all, is understood as referring to a living person's mental activities, and the word 'soul' – which is, in fact, seldom used nowadays – is understood to cover his spiritual activities. The body is seen as basic to both. No philosopher today would take part in such a speculation as that offered by Descartes in the seventeenth century, that the mind was connected to the body in the pineal gland just behind the brain.

What the average man has granted is that, when he dies, he is in no fit state to enter eternal glory without any delay. Neither very righteous nor very wise, neither a martyr nor a philosopher, he does not see himself as a body or a soul which it would be easy to make perfect. From this instinctive humility has come the theory that when the body dies the soul is sent back to inhabit another body. If the previous life has been good, that body will be superior to the last one. Thus retribution (the law of *karma*) operating after death solves the problem of why in any one life the good and the evil do not seem to be rewarded adequately. It has often been taught that there is a fixed number of souls in the world, endlessly reborn. But the hope has also been held out to the weary that there are a few whose merits, piled up over many hundreds or thousands of these lives in different bodies, eventually win for them a place in eternal bliss and even absorption into the One. This 'transmigration' or 'reincarnation' of souls, with the consequence that the good man could raise himself from life to life, has been the central doctrine of the religion of India, but it has not been confined to Hinduism. The idea was found in Ancient Greece, and the writings of Plato include poetic speculations about it. Many millions more have accepted this idea than have believed in the Old Testament's resurrection of the body or in Plato's immortality of the soul.

And to many millions, the unending cycle of reincarnations on earth has seemed a nightmare grimmer than the half-life of Sheol. Gautama the Buddha won his place as the founder of a noble 'way' by his protest against the Hindu idea of the inevitability of reincarnation – and against the Hindu practice of regarding the division of society into castes as sacred because each member of a caste, high or low, had earned that position in some previous incarnation. Gautama taught that the self was *not* indestructible. There was a secret of how to escape from the cycle of life, and Gautama revealed that secret. It was to free oneself of all passions, of all that bound one to existence, by withdrawal from everyday life, by self-denial and by meditations. Any disciple could liberate himself in this way if he had the will, whatever his position in society, but it would help greatly if he joined the Buddhist order of monks, the *Sangha*. Thus he could find release from life into *Nirvana* or Nothingness, as when the flame of a candle was blown out. The good man could raise himself to the extinction of his individuality. By arduous spiritual exercises he could kill his own soul. Reincarnation set the problem to which Buddhism provided the answer.

In the twentieth century, both the problem and the answer seem increasingly incredible. The pressure against the doctrine of reincarnation has not come mainly from intellectual arguments. (Indeed, some competent twentieth-century philosophers have been attracted to these Eastern solutions of the riddle of existence.) The pressure has come from a more formidable source – from the nature of modern life.

It is significant that in the West, the idea of reincarnation never caught on widely. The belief of the West – influenced by Israel, by Greece and by other sources – has been that each individual matters. He is that one, and not someone else. How then could he become someone else after the death of his body? The idea of continuity between the individual as he now is and as he will be immortally, has been difficult enough for the West to understand, without raising the intolerable complication of supposing that the individual will after death become another mortal. This idea of personality has become a key element in the whole Western way of thinking and living, and as Western influence has spread all over the world it has proved inevitable that modernization encourages individualism. And together with this Western or modern emphasis on the individual has come the emphasis on this life as good. Hinduism and Buddhism had their cheerful sides, of course – but their background was suffering, and their spiritual foundations were pessimistic. Jewish, Greek and other elements contributed to the growth of a happier idea in the West; and here again, the impact of this Western idea has been part of the modernization of many countries.

So the questions have been pressed on Asia in our time. If each individual is unique, how can he be reborn as another? And if life can be enjoyable, why should its continuance on earth be regarded as the great disaster? There are signs that Hinduism and Buddhism may be beginning to reinterpret their belief in reincarnation (as the religions which are indebted to Zoroaster are beginning to reinterpret their belief in resurrection). It is certainly a fact that many Asians have already abandoned this belief.

6 *Is Death the End?*

If glory, as this has been imagined in the past, is not to be the eternal destiny of the good man, is death?

Our age of scepticism itself recoils from the finality of death. We are sceptical enough to know that the hope of the nineteenth-century George Eliot is not really much consolation to us:

> O may I join the choir invisible
> Of those immortal dead who live again
> In minds made better by their presence . . . ![7]

For we know that for one 'immortal dead' giant, such as Socrates, who is remembered, history can show a hundred million people who, so far as this world is concerned, have perished as if they had never been born, like the waves in the middle of the ocean (to use two poetic expressions of the dismal truth). We are sceptical enough to know that what we do or are on this planet is so fragmentary, and so frustrated, that it can have real meaning only if it becomes part of a reality which is stronger than death. If no such reality exists, then our lives are now fundamentally – and in the end entirely – meaningless in an accidental universe. Many of our age's own sceptical thinkers have said so. Such is the dark background of many modern plays, films and novels. And we rebel.

In the eighteenth century, the philosopher Immanuel Kant criticized all previous proofs of the existence of God and immortality. Keeping within the limits of pure reason, he insisted that there could be no such proofs. But he also said that our reason must be 'practical'. We are moral beings, and we know that we ought to do right, whatever the immediate consequences. Indeed, we know that we ought to do right although the consequences often disappoint us. And Kant believed that the conscience was itself a witness to the reality which pure reason could not prove – the reality of a God who rewarded the good immortally. Kant believed that our 'practical' reason therefore required 'the endless duration of the existence and personality of the same rational being'.[8]

As a *proof* of immortality, Kant's argument is usually judged to be as defective as its predecessors, for it is possible that our wish for morality always to be rewarded may not be granted in reality. 'What ought to be' is not the same as 'what is'. But Kant's argument does have this strength: if not a proof, it is a wish. It reminds an age of scepticism, when pure reason seems to have demolished all the myths about survival, resurrection or immortality, that from his earliest days man has believed – or at least, has often said – that his life could not make sense without some kind of life after death. From the Greek philosopher's idea of immortality to the Eastern sage's doctrine of *karma*, a vision of a future life has usually been thought essential to a vision of the meaning of history. In his *Phaedo*, Plato declared that 'those who philosophize aright study nothing but dying and being dead'. That is obviously rhetoric; yet wisdom has usually been associated with an attitude to death – accepting death, defying it, denying its reality or claiming its conquest. 'Death, be not proud . . . !' At the end of his great series of Gifford Lectures on *The Varieties of Religious Experience* (1902), William James said: 'Religion, in fact, for the majority of our own race, *means* immortality, and nothing else.' That is probably not quite true, but it is certainly true that most people have associated the meaning of life with the idea of God or gods, and the idea of God or gods with survival, resurrection or immortality for at least some of mankind.[9]

God, as William James put it, is 'the producer of immortality'. God, as the Bible pictured it, will not allow man to claim as his right the fruit of the tree of eternal life (Gen. 3.22), but he may in the end offer a dead man that fruit, as he once breathed life into a man formed 'of dust' (Gen. 2.7). Is this belief, in its essence as old as history, entirely mistaken? Because of the supreme importance of this question, for many of us in the twentieth century the debate continues and at its centre is the question about God.

NOTES

1. See the essay by Eric Rhode on 'Death in Twentieth Century Fiction' in *Man's Concern with Death*, London: Hodder and Stoughton and New York: McGraw-Hill, 1968.

2. Stephen Findlay, *Immortal Longings*, London: Gollancz, 1961, p. 168.

3. Louis Macneice, *An Ecologue for Christmas*.

4. Corliss Lamont, *The Illusion of Immortality*, London: Watts and Co., 1952, Preface to Second Edition.

5. Even the Revised Standard Version (1952) says 'Redeemer'.

6. *Tractatus Logico-Philosophicus*, 6.431 and 6.1411.

7. The brilliant lady known as George Eliot, the novelist and translator, was a major figure, representative of those who sought to combine a scepticism about religious beliefs with adherence to much of Christian morality. The account by F. W. H. Myers of a conversation in a garden in Cambridge 'on an evening of rainy May' in 1873 is deservedly famous. On that occasion George Eliot, 'taking as her text the three words which have been used so often as the inspiring trumpet-call of men, – the words *God, Immortality, Duty*, – pronounced, with terrible earnestness, how inconceivable was the *first*, how unbelievable the *second*, and yet how peremptory and absolute the *third*'. For an introduction to this post-Christian movement of English thought, see Basil Willey, *Nineteenth Century Studies* (London: Chatto and Windus, 1949).

8. Immanuel Kant, *Critique of Practical Reason* (1788).

9. A number of books written at the time of the first world war had this theme and have not lost their value. The best was J. H. Leckie, *The World to Come and Final Destiny*, Edinburgh: T. and T. Clark, 1918.

2 The New Testament

1 *The Message of Jesus*

What has Christianity to say now about this mystery of death? If we are to study the Christian contribution to the debate honestly, we ought to note that Christians have said many things which seem utterly incredible to modern men. But instead of wasting space on criticizing the past, we must try to be constructive, interpreting for ourselves the experience which lies behind the long and often tragic story of Christian theology. And first we must study the New Testament.

The figure who stands at the beginning of the Christian tradition might be expected to be a man acutely conscious of the approach of death and eternity, a man who taught his fellows to fear the wrath of the eternal God, and above everything else a man who taught that God was good and that heaven with him would be an unutterable glory. We do indeed find that Jesus was remembered as such a teacher. His story about the rich man was remembered, for example. 'But God said to him, "You fool, this very night you must surrender your life; you have made your money – who will get it now?" ' (Luke 12.20). So was his story about Lazarus. 'One day the poor man died and was carried away by the angels to be with Abraham' (Luke 16.22). So were his warnings. 'Fear him . . . who is able to destroy both body and soul in hell!' (Matt. 10.28). 'Then he will say to those on his left hand, "The curse is upon you; go from my sight to the eternal fire which is ready for the devil and his angels. . . ." And they will go away to eternal punishment, but the righteous will enter eternal life' (Matt. 25.41, 46).

But all this was not what excited the contemporaries and the first followers of Jesus. Indeed, most of this message was the stock in trade of most Jewish rabbis. The need to prepare for death had always been a part of Jewish piety, and in the first century AD the belief in a resurrection after death seems to have been accepted by all except the most conservative minority, the Sadducees. This small but powerful group clung to the written law in the Old Testament, and excluded later beliefs such as the Book of Daniel's. Life after death meant to them Sheol, and Sheol only. 'The Sadducees deny that there is any resurrection, or angel, or spirit, but the Pharisees accept them' (Acts 23.8). The other Jews, however, believed that the equality of all the dead in Sheol was not enough. There must be distinctions among the dead, between the righteous in 'Abraham's Bosom' (a superior suburb of Sheol) and the wicked in 'eternal punishment'; and there must be a resurrection in order to reward all and reveal everything. So Jesus, like St Paul after him, sided with the Pharisees and the majority.

A rabbi who confined himself to this message would surely not have been crucified. Why, then, was Jesus crucified? He is reported as believing that he must 'surrender his life as a ransom for many' (Mark 10.45); his suffering was to be the price of their freedom. There is, however, no evidence that Jesus regarded his death as a sacrifice to appease the justice of God, or as necessary to make God's forgiveness possible. On the contrary, the evidence suggests that Jesus accepted his death as the price to be paid for alarming the Jewish religious authorities and the Roman political authorities by his central message – a message which would seem blasphemy to Jews and high treason to Romans. To deliver this message, and to illustrate it by his actions, was his life's work.

What, then, was his central message? Jesus was a prophet who announced that *the last things were just about to begin, or were actually now beginning*. The people around him understood him to some extent, for they interpreted this message in the light of other teachings which were in the air at the time. In Palestine, the last century BC and the first century AD were (according to the evidence which has survived) a period when many people expected the end of history to come within a few years. The hopes of the Maccabean rebels had been disappointed, like the hopes of prophets such as Isaiah or Second Isaiah previously. Under the rule of alien kings, and finally under the empire of Rome, the Palestinian Jews had lost all hope of national prosperity by natural means – although many individual Jews in the Dispersion, and some in the Holy Land itself, lived comfortably. If the hopes of Jewish national history were to be fulfilled, it must be as a result of divine intervention in a tragic time. A new age must begin. The Lord God of Israel must reveal himself as king over all the nations. This was the 'Apocalyptic' hope ('Apocalypse' comes from the Greek for 'Revelation'). Many Apocalyptic writings survive and have been studied minutely by scholars in this century. And scholars recognize – as the first hearers of Jesus recognized – the existence of many similarities between the Apocalyptic hopes and the 'good news' which Jesus preached. It was to an expectant Palestine that the message was first delivered. 'After John had been arrested, Jesus came into Galilee proclaiming the Gospel of God: "The time has come; the kingdom of God is upon you; repent, and believe the Gospel" ' (Mark 1. 14–15).

The Apocalyptic teachings were full of details about what would happen when God revealed himself as king in this miraculous way. Jesus does not seem to have joined in this guessing game, but for all his reticence he does seem to have had certain clear expectations about the new age which he was inaugurating. It would be an age in which the will of God was done by men on earth as it already was by the angels in heaven. It would be an age of joy and feasting. Jesus based a number of his parables on this popular hope. His table-fellowship with his disciples and with sinners, and his mysterious feeding of the thousands in the wilderness, could be understood as acted parables. It was believed that he had said at his last supper, 'I tell you this: never again shall I drink from the fruit of the vine until that day when I drink it new in the kingdom of God' (Mark 14.25; see Luke 22.18).

It would be an age of the Holy Spirit (as had been promised in Joel 2.28). Apparently, Jesus felt the power of this Holy Spirit already at work in him, he promised this gift of God to his disciples, and he promised the gift to all who prayed for it to the heavenly Father. *And it would be an age of resurrection.* We cannot be sure of the exact words which Jesus used about his own future, but he seems to have expected a vindication by God after his death; and, from the Book of Daniel onwards, the Apocalyptic hope was clear at this point. The vindication in the kingdom of God would be a physical resurrection from the dead. Meanwhile, the gift of the Holy Spirit as the kingdom of God came would enable Jesus and his disciples to conquer the demons who caused diseases, and to conquer death itself. The healing miracles were signs that the kingdom was already beginning. 'Go and tell John what you hear and see: the blind recover their sight, the lame walk, the lepers are clean, the deaf hear, the dead are raised to life, the poor are hearing the good news' (Matt. 11.5). 'If it is by the Spirit of God that I drive out the devils, then be sure the kingdom of God has already come upon you' (Matt. 12.28).

The words and the work of Jesus were, therefore, interpreted by himself and by many of his hearers as both the announcement and the inauguration of the coming kingdom of God, to which the whole Apocalyptic movement had looked forward. This summary of the gospels rests not on any isolated text, but on the whole evidence of them and of the rest of the New Testament, as discussed during our century freely and exhaustively by the international community of scholars. Particular texts may be ambiguous – for example, the phrase which has encouraged much spiritualizing in Christianity but for which the translation usually preferred by modern scholars is 'the kingdom of God is *among* you' (Luke 17.21). Jesus told parables about the kingdom of God growing hiddenly, but it is now uncertain whether he was referring to the future or (more probably) to the long preparation in the past for that crisis of his contemporaries. Jesus also seems to have uttered prophecies about the imminent heightening of the crisis, but it is now uncertain whether he or his followers were responsible for the words in the gospels about the fall of Jerusalem and other coming woes. However, what matters more than any uncertainty about such details is the clarity of the central message. Parable after parable, saying after saying, warned the hearers to 'read the signs of the times', to acknowledge the crisis then confronting them, to repent while there was still the opportunity, and so to enter the kingdom of God.

Some students have claimed that the message of Jesus concerned the inauguration of this kingdom in his own words and work, but not its future fulfilment in God's world-transforming intervention. (This is the argument that Jesus taught a 'realized eschatology', in the theological jargon.) However, such attempts have had to be abandoned by almost all modern scholars, in the face of the evidence of the New Testament. Here again it is not a question of isolated texts; it is a matter of doing simple justice to the clear thrust of many passages. If we want to quote texts (which may have been edited or constructed by the Christians), texts are available. 'I tell you this: there are some of those standing here who will not taste death before they have seen the kingdom of God already come in power' (Mark 9.1). 'When you see all this happening, you may know that the end is near, at the very door. I tell you this: the present generation will live to see it all. Heaven and earth will pass away; my words will never pass away' (Mark 13.29–31). But since the futurity of the kingdom of God in the teaching of Jesus is not really in dispute nowadays, it is pointless to multiply texts. It is more to the point to remember that the rest of the New Testament thrills with the same hope. All the evidence which we have suggests that the Christians of the first century expected their age to be replaced soon by the new age, in which the kingdom of God would come 'in power' on earth as in heaven; and that they believed that their Lord had promised this.

What, then, was the experience behind this passionate conviction about the coming new age, which the first Christians learned from their Lord? It was not the experience of quiet prayer to the God who would judge all men in eternity, although as devout Jews Jesus and his disciples had this experience. Their key experience seems, rather, to have been an overwhelming excitement because God was acting in a new way. God was using Jesus as his 'finger' (Luke 11.20). It is reported that when some of his disciples jubilantly told Jesus that even the demons had submitted to them, Jesus replied, 'I watched how Satan fell, like lightning, from the sky'. The report continues: 'At that moment Jesus exulted in the Holy Spirit . . . and turning to his disciples he said, "Everything is entrusted to me by my Father. . . ."' (Luke 10.17–22). This experience was interpreted as evidence for the beginning of the new age which so many at that time expected in the Apocalyptic hope. Surely God would crown his new work! And surely he would do it soon!

Jesus, however, has been remembered as none of the Apocalyptic writers has been. Although the kingdom of God has never yet come 'on earth as in heaven', the Jesus who taught the Lord's prayer has been worshipped by many millions. All those who heard him tasted death. His own last words, according to the earliest of the gospels, were: 'My God, my God, why hast thou forsaken me?' (Mark 15.34). But his words have not passed away.

2 *The Experience of Christians*

How can we account for the survival of Christianity after the disappointment of its original hope that the Kingdom of God would come soon? The answer to this crucial question takes us to the very heart of our subject in this book, for it shows us a Jesus who, while clothing his central message in the Apocalyptic hope familiar to himself and his hearers, rose superior to the Apocalyptic follies. And so it shows us a Jesus who has a message for the twentieth century.

The answer to our question comes through meditation on the great paradox in the character of Jesus, as this character is reflected in the gospels and the other documents of the New Testament. Jesus is movingly poor and humble – the Servant, the Man for Others and the Man for God. He was remembered as the man who would wash feet. Yet he is also extraordinarily sure of his place in the triumph of God – he changes the law which was believed to be divine, he forgives sins, he teaches that people's eternal destiny depends on their obedience to his call and command. He comes before us *incognito* – yet his whole way of teaching and acting implies a claim to be more than a prophet and more than a rabbi, and the great titles given to him (Messiah, Son of Man, Son of God, Image of God, Word of God, Lord and God) became inevitable. So it is in his proclamation that the last things are coming.

He did not stake everything on the accuracy of the date or any other detail in his picture of the last things. The New Testament which reports his conviction that the end of this age was near in time tells us that even at the height of his prophetic enthusiasm Jesus urged caution. Words in St Mark's gospel are paralleled elsewhere: 'Then, if anyone says to you, "Look, here is the Messiah", or, "Look there he is", do not believe it!' (Mark 13.21). His disciples were left without accurate information about the future: 'You do not know when the moment comes' (Mark 13.33). Perhaps, indeed, the end would be some time ahead, for 'before the end the Gospel must be proclaimed to all nations' (Mark 13.10). And Jesus seems to have qualified his own prophecies by the admission that he himself did not know precisely when the end would come. St Mark records an admission which many scholars believe reflects the mind of the historical Jesus. (Since it is a confession of ignorance made by their Lord, the early Christians would not have invented it. Since it is closely connected with an expectation that all the prophecies would come true before that generation had ended, it was not part of any attempt by St Mark to play down the emphasis on the kingdom coming soon.) The admission is: 'But about that day or that hour no one knows, not even the angels in heaven, not even the Son; only the Father' (Mark 13.32).

It was his humility before the Father, his conviction that knowledge (like goodness) belonged fully to the Father alone, while he was confident that the Father was using his life to speed the crisis, that saved Jesus from the fate of the Apocalyptic manufacturers of detailed predictions which history soon proved false. This strange humility of the Lord was remembered by the Christians whose own expectations were disappointed.

However, a cautious humility was – certainly – not the only note in the symphony of the teaching of Jesus. Clearly, he did stake everything on his claim that *something* unprecedented would occur in the very near future, while he admitted that he could not give detailed predictions. And nothing would have saved Jesus from the fate of the many 'impostors . . . claiming to be messiahs or prophets' (Mark 13.22), if *nothing* at all had happened. He would have joined 'Theudas, claiming to be somebody', and 'Judas the Galilean at the time of the census' – frustrated rebels whom a wise man such as Gamaliel could ridicule (Acts 5.36, 37). And the words of Jesus were written down by men who believed that something *had* happened to vindicate them, although they also knew that history had not ended in the thirties of the first century.

What, then, was this 'something'? It was the resurrection of Jesus, followed by the gift of the Holy Spirit to his disciples. We, too, can be sure that something happened – although we cannot be sure exactly what it was.

In his gospel and in his Book of the Acts of the Apostles, St Luke claims that the resurrection of Jesus from the dead was physical, leaving behind an empty tomb, and that the gift of the Holy Spirit, first in Jerusalem and on each later occasion, was dramatically miraculous. Thus the prophecies of Daniel and Joel, as well as the hopes of Jesus himself, had been fulfilled; the last things, ushering in the kingdom of God, had clearly begun. The rest of the New Testament does not contradict this claim. Indeed, St Paul's first letter to the Christians in Corinth shows that this claim had been part of the Church's accepted tradition when he had first visited Corinth, within twenty years of the alleged events in Jerusalem. 'I handed on to you the facts which had been imparted to me: that Christ died . . . ; that he was buried; that he was raised to life on the third day . . . ; and that he appeared to Cephas, and afterwards to the Twelve, . . . to over five hundred of our brothers at once, . . . to James, and afterwards to all the apostles' (I Cor. 15.3–7). The Corinthians were also expected to know that one Christian had been granted 'by the one Spirit gifts of healing, and another miraculous powers; another has the gift of prophecy, and another ability to distinguish true spirits from false; yet another has the gift of ecstatic utterance of different kinds, and another the ability to interpret it' (I Cor. 12.9, 10).

However, the whole emphasis was not put on the physical nature of the resurrection or on the miraculous nature of the Holy Spirit. Thus St Paul stressed with much passion his authority as an apostle who could witness to the resurrection, although there was no claim that he had seen the risen body of Jesus on the road to Damascus. 'God . . . chose to reveal his Son to me and through me' (Gal. 1.16). 'Am I not an apostle? Did I not see Jesus our Lord?' (I Cor. 9.1). 'He appeared even to me' (I Cor. 15.8). St Paul also, when listing 'the harvest of the Spirit', put his emphasis on qualities of character: 'love, joy, peace, patience, kindness, goodness, fidelity, gentleness, self-control' (Gal. 5.22). He put spiritual gifts before wonder-working, the mind before the miracles. 'One man, through the Spirit, has the gift of wise speech, while another, by the power of the same Spirit, can put the deepest knowledge into words. Another, by the same Spirit, is granted faith. . . .' (I Cor. 12.8, 9). 'I would rather speak five intelligible words . . . than thousands of words in the language of ecstasy' (I Cor. 14.19).

45

Alternative attitudes are therefore possible when we interpret the experience of the first generation of Christians.

On the one hand, it is possible to accept the accuracy (or, at least, the substantial accuracy) of the account which the New Testament gives of the resurrection of Jesus and the gifts of the Holy Spirit. According to this view, St Luke, for example, was soberly recounting history when he wrote his narrative. 'There he was, standing among them . . . "Touch me and see; no ghost has flesh and bones as you can see that I have" . . . They offered him a piece of fish they had cooked, which he took and ate before their eyes' (Luke 24.36–43). 'And there appeared to them tongues like flames of fire, dispersed among them and resting on each one. And they were all filled with the Holy Spirit and began to talk in other tongues, as the Spirit gave them power of utterance. . . . The crowd gathered, all bewildered because each one heard the apostles talking in his own language' (Acts 2.3–6).

On the other hand, it is possible to say that St Luke, for example, was using poetic symbols in the attempt to account for the origins of the new Christian experience. According to this second view, the appearances of the risen Jesus were probably psychic phenomena, so that it is illuminating to compare the narratives about them with the records of the Society for Psychical Research; and the ecstasies of the first Christians were probably hysterical phenomena, brought about by their high state of excitement, so that it is interesting to compare their 'speaking with tongues' with modern medical evidence. This second view explains the stories of the empty tomb and the flesh and bones of the risen body, and the report of the ability of the apostles to speak many foreign languages without any instruction, as legends which grew up as a result of these phenomena.

If it was possible for St Paul to claim to have seen the risen Lord without seeing his flesh and bones, and if it was possible for him to ignore the story of the apostles' languages, it does not seem necessary for us to take completely and literally the first of the two views which were just stated, if we are to press on with our attempt to study the experience of the first Christians. Indeed, it seems wisest to confess to a good deal of agnosticism about *exactly* what happened within the first-century 'something', while noting that the whole New Testament, and the whole history of the Christian Church, bear witness to the reality of this something. 'If it was "vision",' the Archbishop of Canterbury has said, 'it was "vision" created not from within themselves but by Jesus in his own objective impact on them; and . . . if it was "bodily", it was so with a big difference as belonging to a new order of existence.'[1]

The experience of the resurrection and the Holy Spirit was the experience of the coming of the Kingdom of God within the lives of many of those who had first heard the words of Jesus. And this experience did not end quickly, although the Christians agreed that the body of Jesus could be seen no more and that miracles grew less dramatic. The good news of the 'signs' of the first Easter and the first Whitsun was spread by the apostles. The Christian Church was built on this foundation; and in the Church, other 'signs' followed. One of the latest documents in the New Testament shows that Christians then hoped that the 'signs' in their day would be greater than any of the 'signs' before the death of Jesus. According to St John, Jesus promised that 'he who has faith in me will do what I am doing; and he will do greater things still because I am going to the Father. Indeed, anything you ask in my name I will do. . . .' (John 14.12, 13). The same passage in St John makes clear the emphasis on truth and love among these 'signs' of the continuing work of Jesus. Whether or not the historical Jesus made such promises, the experience of the first Christian century is reflected impressively here.

3 *The Changing Hopes of the Christians*

This experience remained with the Christians as the greatest fact of their lives, and it carried them through the disappointment of many of their hopes.

The New Testament makes it clear enough what these

hopes were. They were hopes that the kingdom of God would come fully in its power and glory on earth, and with it Jesus himself as the visible Lord of all men. '*Marana tha* – Come, O Lord!' Thus St Paul quoted the Church's prayer in the language spoken by Jesus, Aramaic (I Cor. 16.22). 'From heaven we expect our deliverer to come, the Lord Jesus Christ', wrote St Paul in one of the last of his surviving letters. 'He will transfigure the body belonging to our humble state, and give it a form like that of his own resplendent body. . . . The Lord is near; have no anxiety' (Phil. 3.20, 21; 4.6). The last of the surviving gospels to be accepted by the Church contained a promise that 'the time is coming when all who are in the grave shall hear his voice and move forth: those who have done right will rise to life; those who have done wrong will rise to hear their doom' (John 5.28, 29). And it concluded with the thought that Jesus could, if he so wished, make John 'wait until I come' (John 21.22). The New Testament ends with a promise and a prayer: ' "Yes, I am coming soon!" *Amen.* Come, Lord Jesus!' (Rev. 22.20).

The Lord Jesus did *not* come soon, bringing the kingdom of God, in the way they expected. Experience made one Christian anticipate the objection: 'Where now is the promise of his coming?' (II Pet. 3.4). But that Christian also said that the objection would come 'in the last days,' and would soon look foolish (II Peter 3.3.). Even if the last days were delayed, this Christian exhorted his friends not to lose sight of the fact that 'with the Lord one day is like a thousand years and a thousand years like one day'. They were never to forget that the whole universe was to break up in a great conflagration; they were always to 'look eagerly for the coming of the Day of God and work to hasten it on' (II Pet. 3.8, 11, 12). And we may assume that this Christian's faith would not have been destroyed, if he had been persuaded that instead of fire in the heavens the stars would grow cold. Detailed expectations might be revised, but the basic faith remained firm, for it had been founded on an experience which was an ever-present fact. The

New Testament bears witness to this by its presentation of the crisis of faith which resulted from the delay in 'his coming'. That presentation is undramatic. We might have expected the documents to record agonized controversies and heart-searchings over the time-table of the kingdom, as they do over the status of the Gentiles in the Church. But no: the passage just quoted is the sharpest reference to this problem in the New Testament.

The rest of the New Testament shows a process of quiet restatement in response to the challenge. St Paul, writing in or about AD 50, had told the Thessalonians 'as the Lord's word' that some of them would be alive when the Lord descended from heaven. 'First the Christian dead will rise, then we who are left alive shall join them, caught up in clouds to meet the Lord in the air' (I Thess. 4.15–17). But even then there was a note of caution. 'About dates and times, my friends, we need not write to you, for you know perfectly well that the Day of the Lord comes like a thief in the night' (I Thess. 5.1). When he came to write to the Corinthians, about five years later, St Paul had grown convinced that the resurrected bodies of the dead would *not* be the same flesh as the flesh which had been buried, and the bodies of those surviving on earth at the time of the general resurrection would also have to be changed, for 'flesh and blood can never possess the kingdom of God, and the perishable cannot possess immortality' (I Cor. 15.35–52). He still believed that 'the time we live in will not last long' (I Cor. 7.29), so 'we shall not all die' (I Cor. 15.51), but to say this was to 'unfold a mystery', and it seems to have mattered more that 'in the Lord your labour cannot be lost' (I Cor. 15.58).

By the time he wrote to Corinth again (at an unknown date), St Paul had changed his emphasis again. 'We do not lose heart! Though our outward humanity is in decay, yet day by day we are inwardly renewed. Our troubles are slight and short-lived; and their outcome an eternal glory which outweighs them far' (II Cor. 4.16, 17). He urged Christians to fix their eyes on 'the things that are unseen', which are 'eternal' (II Cor. 4.18). Death now seemed a fearful possibility for St Paul and his fellow-Christians: 'We groan indeed, . . . we are oppressed because we do not want to have the old body stripped off' (II Cor. 5.4). But already the new, spiritual body existed to clothe Christians. Perhaps this was an individual body, waiting in heaven; or perhaps (but this is the more unlikely interpretation of St Paul's mysterious words) it was the Church, the Body of Christ on earth and in heaven. 'For we know that if the earthly frame that houses us today should be demolished, we possess a building which God has provided – a house not made by human hands, eternal, and in heaven' (II Cor. 5.1). So, despite any groaning, Christians could be confident. 'We . . . would rather leave our home in the body and go to live with the Lord' (II Cor. 5.8). And when writing to Philippi, St Paul could imply that he had overcome any lingering expectation that he would be spared death – and also any lingering fear of it. 'What I should like is to depart and be with Christ; that is better by far' (Phil. 1.23).

The fourth gospel was based on mature Christian experience, at the turn of the first and second Christian centuries. It supremely illustrated the confidence that a Christian could 'be with,' or could 'dwell in,' Jesus *even before his death*. St John the Evangelist wished to assure Christians that 'you *have* eternal life' (I John 5.13). And he did not hesitate to express this as the Lord's word – just as St John the Divine had not hesitated to compose a speech from the Lord, in order to express his faith in that Lord who already had eternal glory: 'Do not be afraid. I am the first and the last, and I am the living one; for I was dead and now I am alive for evermore, and I hold the keys of death and Hades' (Rev. 1.17, 18).

To each St John, the Evangelist and the Divine (and to St Paul and others also), it was as if Jesus did speak through the developing experience of the Church, and through its developing interpretation. The historical Jesus had hoped (it was believed) that those standing by him would not taste death. The eternal Jesus, alive in heaven and in the

Church on earth, could now proclaim that, whether they lived or died, those who believed in him had *already* passed 'from death to life' (John 5.24). Christians heard this message in the Church. Sometimes they heard it through abnormal experiences such as the ecstatic trance which St John the Divine reported from the Roman concentration camp on the island of Patmos. But mostly Christians heard the message of eternal life through their quieter experiences of life in the Church. They heard it in their worship; and in their common life as Christians, they slowly learned more and more about the power of their risen, eternal Lord. They saw this Jesus in each other's faces. It was the discovery of Christians as the Body of Christ – the discovery which St Paul had made on the Damascus road ('I am Jesus, whom you are persecuting': Acts 9.5). And with this discovery of new life in each other went the discovery of eternal life for the whole Christian brotherhood. 'We for our part have crossed over from death to life,' wrote St John in the first of his letters which have survived, and he added: 'This we know, because we love our brothers' (I John 3.14).

So we hear the great 'words of eternal life' (John 6.68) in the fourth gospel. 'Whoever drinks the water that I shall give him will never suffer thirst any more. The water that I shall give him will be an inner spring always welling up for eternal life' (John 4.14). 'Whoever eats my flesh and drinks my blood possesses eternal life, and I will raise him up on the last day' (John 6.54). Christian believers who have been baptized, and who feed on Jesus in the Eucharist, belong for ever to the Lord and therefore belong for ever to the life. 'If anyone obeys my teaching he shall never know what it is to die' (John 8.51). 'I give them eternal life and they shall never perish; no one shall snatch them from my care' (John 10.28). They know that 'this is the true God, this is eternal life' (I John 5.21). 'This *is* eternal life,' says St John's Jesus in his prayer: 'to know thee who alone art truly God, and Jesus Christ whom thou hast sent' (John 17.3).

Eternal life here and now, given and revealed by Jesus Christ, does not exclude the resurrection and the Revelation, the Apocalypse, on the last day; but it, rather than the Jewish belief in the final resurrection, is now taught by St John as the distinctively Christian belief. Martha speaks of the previous hope when she says to Jesus about her brother Lazarus: 'I know that he will rise again at the resurrection on the last day.' And St John shares this belief in the coming end, giving it a Christian turn. 'Even now, my children, dwell in him, so that when he appears we may be confident and unashamed before him at his coming . . . when . . . we shall be like him, because we shall see him as he is' (I John 2.28, 3.2). But in the fourth gospel, the Jesus who has wept for Lazarus reveals what is thrillingly new and Christian, as the good news for Lazarus now: '*I am* the resurrection and *I am* life' (John 11.25).

If the experience which Christians already enjoyed suggested that they already had eternal life, it followed in St John's thought that the most important of the promises of Jesus had already been fulfilled. While not denying that Jesus would appear again finally, St John saw that the time between the prophecies of Jesus and his return was even shorter than the most Apocalyptic of Christians had hoped. The time was, in fact, already past; it was the time between the first Good Friday and the first Easter Day. 'A little while, and you see me no more,' says the Jesus of St John at his last supper; 'again, a little while and you will see me . . . I shall see you again, and then you will be joyful, and no one shall rob you of your joy' (John 16.16, 22). The Christians had grown accustomed to thinking of the visible return of Jesus as his *apokalypsis*, his 'revelation' (e.g. I Cor. 1.7), or as his *parousia*, which was the official visitation of an area by a government official (e.g. I Cor. 15.23). Now St John claimed that what they had already seen was what was most important. Jesus had been revealed to them, and had visited them in his power and his glory, 'late that Sunday evening, when the disciples were together behind locked doors, for fear of Jews'. 'Peace be with you!' the risen Jesus had said. 'Receive the Holy Spirit!' And even those who had never seen that Lord in his Easter glory could still 'believe' and 'dwell in' his presence on earth. St John wrote down his interpretation of Christian experience in order that 'through this faith you may possess eternal life by his name' (John 20.19–31).

4 *The Remaining Problems*

That is an outline of the drama behind the doctrines in the New Testament. It cannot answer all the problems which arise when we try to state the Christian contribution to thought about death in the twentieth century. What it can do is to show that the doctrines arose not in a vacuum but out of the living experience of Jesus and the Christians. Historical criticism of the Bible, which often appears to distress Christians and even to destroy Christianity, can in fact render the great service of uncovering the living reality beneath these documents and their doctrines. Men and women, including some of the best in the whole story of the human race, once wrote those documents, and struggled to teach those doctrines, because of what they had found in their lives. That thought can itself persuade us to take the twentieth-century problems of Christianity more seriously.

The New Testament leaves many of our questions unanswered. It shows why the first Christians believed that 'our Saviour Jesus Christ . . . has broken the power of death and has brought life and immortality to light through the Gospel' (II Tim. 1.10). But it does not explain to us convincingly how death came to have this power. No teaching by Jesus on this subject has survived, and St Paul merely repeats the mythological story of Adam's sin, which somehow 'brought death upon so many' (Rom. 5.15). He repeats also the belief that 'in Adam all men die' (I Cor. 15.22), for death is a punishment for the sin which Adam began. He does not tell us precisely how people after Adam came to share this sin. 'It was through one man that sin entered the world, and through sin death, and thus death pervaded the whole human race, inasmuch as all men have sinned.' St Paul adds that death 'held sway from Adam to Moses, even over those who had not sinned as Adam did, by disobeying a direct command' (Rom. 5.12, 14). Modern questions are simply not answered here.

Nowhere does the New Testament discuss the problem, so agonizing for so many in modern times, of why the heavenly Father, the God who is love and light and in whom there is no darkness at all (I John 1.5, 4.9), who sent Jesus Christ to be the remedy for the defilement of the sins of the whole world (I John 2.2), finds it compatible with his love to sentence the wicked to eternal punishment, so that 'there is such a thing as deadly sin, and I do not suggest that he should pray about that' (I John 5.16). Jesus and the Christians seem to have assumed simply that the good God could do this. They held together without any great strain the two insights: that the good God will triumph, and that human responsibility is terrible. But the two insights were not perfectly united.

Jesus in his teaching about hell appears to have used the conventional picture of Gehenna. This was inspired by the valley of Hinnom (*gey Hinnom*) which lay just to the south of Jerusalem. We are told that King Josiah 'defiled Topheth, which is in the valley of the sons of Hinnom, that no one might burn his son or his daughter as an offering to Molech' (II Kings 23.10). Jeremiah remembered these abominations (Jer. 7.31). In order to discourage any more human sacrifices, the city rubbish dump was established there, and the custom was to put there among all kinds of garbage the corpses of criminals and paupers who did not receive a proper burial in a family cave or other tomb. If the body of the crucified Jesus had not been buried in the cave of Joseph of Arimathea as the gospels say, it would have been thrown into the valley of Hinnom and 'descended into hell' in that sense. Maggots bred in this place, and an ever-burning bonfire was needed. When the conviction grew among the Jews that Sheol, for all its gloom, was too good a fate for the wicked, they imagined the worse fate as being like the valley of Hinnom. The last prophecy collected in the Book of Isaiah at an unknown but late date shows this. 'And they shall go forth and look on the dead bodies of the men that have rebelled against me; for their worm shall not die, their fire shall not be quenched, and they shall be an abhorrence to all flesh' (Isa. 66.24).

We have to assume that this was the picture in the mind of Jesus when he uttered the terrible warnings of which there are echoes in our gospels. 'If your hand is your undoing, cut it off; it is better for you to enter into life maimed than to keep both hands and go to Gehenna and the unquenchable fire . . . where the devouring worm never dies' (Mark 9.43-48). 'Anyone who sneers at his brother will have to answer for it in the fires of Gehenna' (Matt. 5.22). 'Alas for you, lawyers and Pharisees, hypocrites! You travel over sea and land to win one convert; and when you have won him you make him twice as fit for Gehenna as you are yourselves. . . . You snakes, you vipers' brood, how can you escape being condemned to Gehenna?' (Matt. 23.15, 33) Those who were thus condemned would, of course, be bitterly sorry; in the traditional Jewish phrase, they would wail and gnash their teeth (a phrase which occurs six times in St Matthew's gospel, and in Luke 13.28).

We need not, however, assume that those who compared the fate of the wicked with the valley of Hinnom believed that the wicked would live for ever in endless torture from the fire and the worm. The picture was of corpses being destroyed. The maggots were always breeding, but the bodies on which they feasted were not indestructible. The fire was unquenchable, but not necessarily the life. It is significant that the warning is given in one gospel, 'fear him, rather, who, after he has killed, has authority to cast into Gehenna' (Luke 12.5), but becomes in another: 'Fear him, rather, who is able to destroy both soul and body in Gehenna' (Matt. 10.28). Gehenna was, more than anything else, the place of destruction. It may be significant that the rich man who was 'in torment' was thought of as being in Sheol or Hades, not Gehenna (Luke 16.23). It may also be significant that the most bitterly vindictive document in the New Testament, St John the Divine's Apocalypse, does not describe endless tortures for the wicked, although the Devil in the 'lake of fire and sulphur' was to be 'tormented day and night for ever' (Rev. 20.10). 'Then Death and Hades were flung into the lake of fire. This lake of fire is the second death; and into it were flung any whose names were not to be found in the roll of the living' (Rev. 20.15). The most natural interpretation of this admittedly ambiguous text seems to be that even St John the Divine hesitated to imagine the dead being 'tormented day and night for ever'.

Would many go to Gehenna? A tradition among the early Christians was that Jesus had been asked this question, and had refused to guess about numbers. What concerned him was the urgency of a man's decision between life and death. 'Struggle to get in through the narrow door; for I tell you that many will try to enter and not be able' (Luke 13.24). A sterner version of the same warning comes in another gospel. 'Enter by the narrow gate. The gate is wide that leads to perdition, there is plenty of room on the road, and many go that way; but the gate that leads to life is small and the road is narrow, and those who find it are few' (Matt. 7.13, 14). Such an answer raises the further question of how God can bear to refuse the 'many' who will 'try to enter' heaven. For another tradition was that Jesus had said: 'Ask, and you will receive; seek, and you will find; knock, and the door will be opened' (Luke 11.9). We are bound to ask whether the feast in the kingdom of God can completely accord with the triumphant will of God if many knocks at the door are to be disregarded for all eternity. Will God for ever be deaf to the late arrivals who shout, 'Sir, let us in!' (Luke 13.25), 'Sir, sir, open the door for us!' (Matt. 25.11)? We are bound to ask – but we shall not find a clear answer in the Bible.

Instead, the Bible combines its warnings about the fate of the wicked with promises that God's will shall be done 'on earth as in heaven'. The chapter in the Book of Isaiah which pictures Gehenna also pictures, in the immediately preceding verses, the triumph of God in 'the new heaven and the new earth', when 'all flesh shall come to worship before me, says the Lord' (Isa. 66.22–3). The last chapters in the Bible, which picture the 'second death', also declare that in 'a new heaven and a new earth . . . there shall be an end to death, and to mourning and crying and pain' (Rev. 21.1, 4). In St John's gospel, the disciples are told by Jesus: 'I shall draw all men to myself, when I am lifted up from the earth' (John 12.32). And the deepest insight into the mind of Christ is that it is *he* who stands knocking at the door. That door is the will of man. If any man opens the door, Jesus will enter and will accept that man's limited hospitality – before that man becomes the guest of Jesus in the eternal feast (Rev. 3.20).

St Paul saw the difference between the Church and the world, the Gospel and death, as vividly as either of the Johns. But St Paul and his followers have left behind some of the Bible's most assured proclamations of the Gospel as 'healing for all mankind' (Titus 2.11), and some of its most triumphant pictures of the life and glory of all at the 'time of universal restoration' (Acts 3.21). 'God's purpose was to show mercy to all mankind,' the Christians in Rome are reminded in St Paul's most careful theological treatise (Rom. 11.32). 'God raised him to the heights and bestowed on him the name above all names, that at the name of Jesus every knee should bow – in heaven, on earth, and in the depths – and every tongue confess, "Jesus Christ is Lord", to the glory of God the Father' (Phil. 2.10, 11). These words to the Philippians are believed by many scholars to have been based on an early Christian hymn. They proclaim Christ's rule over the angels in heaven, over all mankind on earth and over all the dead in Sheol, Hades or 'the depths'.

The letter to Colossae repeated and expanded this picture. 'Through him God chose to reconcile the whole universe to himself . . . to reconcile all things, whether on earth or in heaven, through him alone' (Col. 1.20). So did the letter to Ephesus. 'He has made known to us his hidden purpose . . . to be put into effect when the time was ripe', the Christians in Ephesus are reminded: 'namely, that the universe, all in heaven and on earth, might be brought into unity in Christ' (Eph. 1.9, 10). An earlier and indisputably Pauline letter says that 'all things' will be subject to Jesus, and Jesus will be made subordinate to God, 'and thus God will be all in all' (I Cor. 15.28). A triumphant new meaning was given by St Paul to the Old Testament's gloomy reference to the plagues of Sheol (above, p. 15): 'O Death, where is your victory? O Death, where is your sting?' (I Cor. 15.55).

The work of Jesus Christ was for the New Testament the key event in this triumph of God. This work was so important that many passages suggest that only those who accepted it for themselves, believed in him and endured in this belief to the end, could be sure of ultimate salvation. A hymn of the early Christians (quoted in II Tim. 2.11–13) expressed this assurance:

> If we died with him, we shall live with him;
> If we endure, we shall reign with him.
> If we deny him, he will deny us.
> If we are faithless, he keeps faith,
>   For he cannot deny himself.

And this promise and warning were traced back to Jesus: 'Whoever then will acknowledge me before men, I will acknowledge him before my Father in heaven; and whoever disowns me before men, I will disown him before my Father in heaven' (Matt. 10.32, 33).

The New Testament, however, also says that Jesus himself shared the belief of his hearers that at the end 'Abraham, Isaac, and Jacob and all the prophets' would be 'in the kingdom of God' (Luke 13.28) and that on his death a poor man could go to 'be with Abraham' (Luke 16.22). These were not disciples. In the New Testament there is, therefore, a speculation that after his death Jesus 'went and made his proclamation to the imprisoned spirits'. They had 'refused obedience long ago, while God waited patiently in the days of Noah' (I Peter 3.19, 20). The exact meaning of this speculation is obscure, but its purpose seems to be to include not only the patriarchs and prophets but all human history within the offer of eternal life. Even the sinners at the time of the Flood, who 'ate and drank and married' without any thought of God's wrath (Luke 17.27), who 'corrupted their way' and filled the earth with violence (Gen. 6.11, 12), could share in the eternal blessings of baptized Christians.

Jesus also declared that 'many will come from east and west to feast with Abraham, Isaac and Jacob in the kingdom of heaven' (Matt. 8.11). The tradition connected that prophecy with the faith of a Gentile centurion in the healing power of Jesus, but St John the Divine extended it to 'every created thing in heaven and on earth and under the earth and in the sea' (Rev. 5.13). All would in the end praise God and 'the Lamb'. So the kings of the earth would bring all their splendour into the final City of God, and the nations would walk in its light (Rev. 21.24). They, too, must have heard the proclamation of Jesus after death, for the Church in St John the Divine's time included no king. St Matthew gives a picture of some of the Gentiles being surprised after death to discover that they had earned the good Christian's reward. Jesus would hold his assize 'with all the nations gathered before him', and he would declare to the righteous: 'You have my Father's blessing; come, enter and possess the kingdom that has been ready for you since the world was made. . . . Anything you did for one of my brothers here, however humble, you did for me' (Matt. 25.31–40).

That parable taught that those who had not been charitable to the 'brothers' of Jesus (probably the phrase originally referred to the Christians) would be condemned. But who in fact could *not* be forgiven? The tradition of the Christians was that those who tortured Jesus to death could be forgiven; only those who were so blind spiritually that they were capable of describing an act of healing as the work of a demon, not of the Holy Spirit, were beyond forgiveness.

'I tell you this: no sin, no slander, is beyond forgiveness for men; but whoever slanders the Holy Spirit can never be forgiven; he is guilty of eternal sin' (Mark 3.28, 29).

Exactly who was, and who would for ever remain, in this appalling condition, worse than those who drove the nails into the hands of the Son of God? These questions, like many others, are not answered by the New Testament. Some reticence marks its references even to Judas Iscariot: he went to his place, 'where he belonged' (Acts 1.25); 'it would be better for that man if he had never been born' (Mark 14.21). We need not ignore the very solemn warnings against the refusal or betrayal of the Gospel, against the refusal of compassion and against spiritual blindness, if we note that the verse added by a later hand to St Mark's gospel represents an over-simplification: 'those who do not believe will be condemned' (Mark 16.17). It is better to conclude with the frank paradox that the God of the New Testament is 'the Saviour of all men – the Saviour, above all, of believers' (I Tim. 4.10).

What would be the state of the blessed in the kingdom of the Father? Here again, the New Testament, because it struggles to express insights into unfathomable mysteries on the basis of earthly experience, uses symbols which are logically incompatible with each other.

Jesus is reported as assuring the dying bandit: 'today you shall be with me in Paradise' (Luke 23.43). 'Paradise' came from the Persian word which was used to describe the garden of a king or nobleman. St Paul recalled across fourteen years that he '(whether in the body or out of it, I do not know – God knows) was caught up into Paradise, and heard words so secret that human lips may not repeat them' (II Cor. 12.3, 4). It seems that he had this Paradise in mind when he desired to die and so be 'with Christ', for such a mystical experience would have shown him the meaning of the belief that God had (in other New Testament words) 'already brought us to life with Christ . . . and raised us up and enthroned us with him in the heavenly realms' (Eph. 2.5, 6). As we have seen, St John claimed eternal life as a present possession; and St John saw Jesus as promising his disciples: 'I shall come again and receive you to myself, so that where I am you may be also' (John 14.3). Here, it seems, Paradise is promised on earth, or at death. But Jesus, St Paul and St John also expected a final resurrection, and St John the Divine worked out an elaborate time-table for this. Would something be missing, then, for the bandit or the saint, in an 'intermediate state' before the glory at the end? Would they be 'naked' when without the bodies of the resurrection? Many have speculated about this, but the idea of an imperfect Paradise has often seemed intolerably illogical.

The impossibility (not merely the undesirability) of taking the details of the New Testament's pictures of heaven literally can be confirmed by trying to draw a unified and coherent illustration of St John the Divine's prophecy of the end. St Paul ended up with the idea of a spiritual body. It is an idea full of poetry – 'sown in humiliation, it is raised in glory; sown in weakness, it is raised in power; sown as an animal body, it is raised as a spiritual body' (I Cor. 15.43, 44). But it is also an illogical idea, like the idea of a square circle. This body of the dead is not to be the same as our flesh on earth; yet it is to be a body, and our flesh which died will be its seed. (St Paul would have thought, in common with his contemporaries, that seed did die in the earth.) Although St Paul assures us that this is a 'senseless question', we cannot avoid continuing to ask: 'How are the dead raised? In what kind of body?' (I Cor. 15.35). But Jesus himself supplied the necessary warning, for (unlike the Apocalyptic dreamers and his own literally minded followers) he taught that life in the age to come would be very different from life in this age.

The life (or death) of this age to come is described in the New Testament as *aionios*, *aion* being the Greek for 'age'. The 'sons of this age' (Luke 16.8) were the worldly or secular men (our word 'secular' comes from the Latin *saeculum*, meaning 'an age'). What, then, would be the life of the age to come? It would be *aionios*. In classical Greek (e.g. Plato) the word meant 'eternal' or 'timeless', and it was used in the Greek Bible to refer to God and to the things of God – 'permanent' things as we might say. Many things in the age to come would be literally ever-lasting. However, biblical thought avoided the idea of a changeless eternity, and instead imagined a good deal of action which would mean change taking place in the age to come – supremely, the activities of worship and the festivities of joy. It is therefore possible that the teaching reported as coming from Jesus did not necessarily imply that the *aionios* sin, the *aionios* fire and the *aionios* punishment would last for ever, without change (Mark 3.29; Matt. 25.41, 46). Instead Gehenna might mean *aionios* destruction, an end which had taken place for ever (II Thess. 1.9).

We may conclude that the men who wrote the New Testament did not claim to understand all the conditions of the age to come, that *aionios* reality which would be the opposite of the secular reality and yet also its fulfilment. St Paul, for example, apparently recalling the Old Testament's promise that the 'former things' would not be remembered when the new heavens and the new earth came (Isa. 65.17), referred to 'the words of Scripture: "things beyond our seeing, things beyond our hearing, all prepared by God for those who love him" ' (I Cor. 2.9). These last things had been revealed to Christians, but only in 'puzzling reflections in a mirror' (I Cor. 13.12). The New Testament, in using the word *aionios* or its equivalents, did not necessarily intend a philosophical teaching about whether the life of the age to come would be intense, long-lived, changeless, everlasting or timeless. These men had no intention of writing an academic treatise on the concepts of time and eternity. They struggled to express insights arising out of an intensely experienced vision of God as the Lord of the present and the future. They were not so precise, or maybe not so clever, as some of those who have commented on them.[2]

We now have an inevitable tendency to separate ideas about eternity from ideas about history. How, then, can we today interpret the symbols used in the New Testament about the age to come?

NOTES

1. A. M. Ramsey, *Introducing the Christian Faith*, London: SCM Press, 1961, p. 60.
2. For the scholarly controversy, see James Barr, *Biblical Words for Time*, London: SCM Press, 1962.

3 Eternity in Christian Faith Today

1 *The God of the Living*

According to the gospels, when Jesus was asked about the resurrection by some of the Sadducees who rejected belief in it, he appealed to the early parts of the Old Testament, which the Sadducees accepted as authoritative. 'You do not know . . . the scriptures . . . ,' he replied. 'Have you never read in the Book of Moses, in the story of the burning bush, how God spoke to him and said, "I am the God of Abraham, the God of Isaac, and the God of Jacob"? God is not God of the dead, but of the living' (Mark 12.18–27; also in Matt. 22.23–33; Luke 20.27–38).

We who do not share the Sadducees' attitude to the story of the burning bush can learn from this story about Jesus. We can learn where the heart of the debate about resurrection or immortality lies. *It lies in the question who 'God' is.* Is 'God' an idea which corresponds with no reality? If there is reality here, does this reality have the power to counteract death? If God has the power, is God's nature such that he has the will?

Jesus affirmed that the reality behind the traditional Hebrew idea of *Yahweh* (God) could rightly be experienced as *Abba*, Father (Mark 14.36; Luke 11.2; quoted in Gal. 4.6; Rom. 8.15). He also taught about God's power. 'Are not sparrows two a penny? Yet without your Father's leave not one of them can fall to the ground' (Matt. 10.29). He also taught about the will of the 'heavenly Father' to care for men. 'As for you, even the hairs of your head have all been counted. So have no fear; you are worth more than many sparrows' (Matt. 10.30, 31). This Father of men was the God who had chosen to be the God of Abraham, Isaac and Jacob. *He could be trusted to raise them from death.* The Sadducees who think otherwise 'do not know either the scriptures or the power of God. . . . You are greatly mistaken' (Mark 12.24, 27).

Many modern people hold that here, at any rate, the Sadducees were not mistaken. The word 'God' often sounds like a meaningless noise in the twentieth century, the time when Nietzsche's nineteenth-century belief that 'God is dead' has become popular. If any significance is attached to the traditional word, 'God' may be regarded as the ultimate reality, indescribable because unknowable. People and things move towards an end, but what the end is no one can tell. Or 'God' may be used as a name for part of the process which is now going on. Some call it evolution, others call it God. Some call it beauty, or truth, or goodness, or love; others prefer the religious name. Or 'God' may be used to refer to a divine being who is thought of as a fighter who sometimes succeeds and sometimes fails. It may be said that reality is a lottery, where chance is the only rule. In such a random universe, God must take his chance like others. Or it may be said that part of reality is, and always will be, disordered or evil; in such a universe the best that God can do is not strong enough to prevent many disasters. Or 'God' may simply be used as the totem of a church, a nation, a political party, a class or a race. The use of the traditional word is intended to give an elevated atmosphere to the conduct which is being advocated on other grounds. In each of these cases the 'God' who is mentioned is, of course, not regarded as stronger than death.

In the twentieth century there has even been an attempt, on quite a large scale, to cut down the importance of 'God' in the message of Jesus. Instead of being a message about his heavenly Father and the coming kingdom, the message of Jesus is reconstructed as a message about human love, or about human freedom, or about human progress, or about the Church, or about himself. If death is considered, it is claimed only that death does not completely destroy the influence of great deeds of love or freedom; that human progress continues, generation after generation; that the Church goes on and Jesus is remembered. It is sometimes added that the death of Jesus is best understood when it is seen as the tragedy of love. A tragedy purges our emotions by pity and terror, as Aristotle said; but it ceases to be a tragedy if it has a happy ending.

Unfortunately for all such theories, however, the Jesus presented by the New Testament (and what other Jesus do we know?) is a man who depends entirely on the power which, he believes, comes to him from the heavenly Father to whom he prays. The Jesus for whose existence there is evidence taught men to trust this Father, and to reshape their whole lives accordingly. He himself seems to have placed his whole trust in the Father. Even in his mortal agony he did not have to confess that he had forsaken God. If the Father whom Jesus regarded in this way was in fact an illusion, and was merely a projection from his memories of the carpenter Joseph, then Jesus should be regarded as a man of his time – a man who if alive now would rightly be regarded as neurotically sick in mind, with only a pathological appeal, and as a fool whom only other fools would follow. Christianity without the Father in fact never commands the respect or the interest of healthy, intelligent people in large numbers over a long time; and this is right.

To share the attitude of Jesus to the Father is a matter of a deliberate choice and a personal faith. This decision cannot be forced on anyone. Nor can it be taken by anyone on behalf of anyone else. Nor can it be evaded by anyone for whom its possibility has been raised seriously. Each person who has really heard this message has to decide for himself whether it is, essentially, *the* truth or *the* illusion.

In this book we are not expected to discuss at length why a modern Christian believes in the God and Father of Jesus Christ. Many books have been written on that subject. None of them fails to reflect a genuine experience, and none of them convinces a person who has not had that experience. The conclusion which a Christian draws is that he is a Christian because God chose him to be one. Why or how God chose him, God knows; but God has given this person an experience which has converted him, while the next person, who may be superior ethically or intellectually or physically, can say that he has never had the experience.

This is the kind of predestination that begins to make sense to the modern Christian – the pre-destination or choice by God of those who are to be Christians, *on earth*. This kind of predestination has a basis in the experience reflected in the New Testament. The early Christians knew that Jesus could say to them, 'You did not choose me: I chose you' (John 15.16). And they attributed this prayer to Jesus: 'I thank thee, Father, Lord of heaven and earth, for hiding these things from the learned and wise, and revealing them to the simple. Yes, Father, such was thy choice' (Matt. 11.25, 26). And the experience of being chosen while unworthy lay behind the writing of one who was never 'simple', St Paul. He could never forget 'how savagely I persecuted the church of God . . . but then in his good pleasure God, who had set me apart from birth and called me through his grace, chose to reveal his Son to me' (Gal. 1.13, 15, 16). That was what made him believe that 'God knew his own before ever they were, and also ordained that they should be shaped to the likeness of his Son, that he might be the eldest among a large family of brothers' (Rom. 8.29). But that experience of being chosen did not make St Paul despair about the ultimate fate of those who were not then Christians.

What we have to do here is to study some of the implications of Christian experience and belief. A Christian option in this debate about death and destiny can be stated, and that must be enough.

We have to deal here with 'the God and Father of our Lord Jesus Christ' (Eph. 1.3). We concentrate on the God in whom Jesus believed, and not any other kind of God suggested by the religious experience of Hindus, for example. And on Jesus Christ's own showing, this is also the God of Abraham, Isaac, Jacob and Moses. Jesus inherited the Old Testament, however radically he interpreted it. The background of his teaching was Jewish, which means that his God was not the God of the Greek, or of any other, philosophers. We are to study the God who is proclaimed in the New and Old Testaments. We have seen how hesitant are the hopes of the Old Testament, but it remains true to say about them, as a great scholar has said: 'The common factor linking all these witnesses to the conquest of death in the life of the individual is that their certainty is built on the gift of fellowship with God here and now.' This scholar goes on to quote Martin Luther, who at this point so vividly encountered the God of the New Testament: 'He with whom God speaks, whether in wrath or in grace, is certainly immortal. The Person of the God who speaks, and the Word of God, show that we are creatures with whom God wills to speak even to eternity and in an immortal manner.'[1] What the sceptic David Hume wrote at the end of his famous essay on the immortality of the soul, with his tongue in his cheek, is profoundly true: 'Nothing could set in a fuller light the infinite obligations which mankind have to Divine revelation, since we find that no other medium could ascertain this great and important truth.'

According to the New and Old Testaments, God gives this revelation only to the person who is humble, who is teachable, who does not demand to be told everything at once, who is prepared to wait, and who is ready to receive more and more of the revelation as he goes on his way through life, step by step. Jesus appealed to the story of the burning bush. In that story, when Moses has taken off his shoes in order to acknowledge that the ground is holy, God gives only three clues to his identity (Ex. 3). First: 'I am the God of your fathers, the God of Abraham, the God of Isaac and the God of Jacob' – the revelation given now is continuous with the past. Second, 'I have seen the affliction of my people . . . I know their sufferings, and I have come down to deliver them' – the revelation is given in a crisis, and in order to meet that crisis. And third, *ehyeh ásher ehyeh*. The usual translation 'I am who I am' is regarded by many modern scholars as inadequate. The Hebrew can also be translated 'I will be what I will be'. 'Most likely, that kind of indefiniteness is expressed,' says Dr Martin Noth, 'which leaves open a large number of possibilities ("I am whatever I mean to be").'[2] Other revelations will be given in future crises, when the God without a name will show who he is by what he does. In the New Testament, Christians remember their beginnings in the historical fact of Jesus, but they also learn from their continuing discipleship in the school of Jesus and from walking in the way of Jesus. St John reflects this experience when he gives the words with which Jesus, the Word of God who 'became flesh', concludes his last appearance to Peter: 'Follow me' (John 21.22).

The God and Father of our Lord Jesus Christ is thus the God who has come, who comes and who will come. He is the historical God, but he is also the God of the future, the God who called Abraham, Moses, Jesus and Peter into an unknown future; and what he gives to us now is simply enough for us to get from the past to the future. If the biblical God is thus the coming God, we must not be surprised to discover that the biblical teaching about the 'age to come' is in fragments relevant to the particular situations of Jews and Christians. Nor must we be surprised to discover that biblical experience perceived and received biblical revelation only gradually. Probably twelve centuries separated the time of Moses from the time of the Book of Daniel's prophecy of the resurrection of the dead. Probably half a century separated St Paul's letters about the resurrection from St John's gospel about eternal life here and now. In the nineteen centuries since St Paul wrote, more has been learned by Christians; and if the human race lasts for as long as the scientists predict, and if the Christian Church lasts with it, two thousand million years of learning lie ahead.

And this is a God who chooses *how* he will act. That is what those who have put their trust in him have learned through their experience of being chosen. The Bible offers no abstract discussion of the nature and limits of God's power. It simply says that God chooses to do what he does, and does what he chooses. The Old Testament declares that Abraham, Isaac and Jacob were who they were because God chose them, and Jesus adds that God still chooses them after their deaths. The New Testament's assurance about eternal life arises from its conviction that 'God is not ashamed to be called their God; for he has a city ready for them' (Heb. 11.16).

2 *Our Enemy, Death*

To the Bible, death is an enemy. It is, indeed, the most obstinate of enemies. 'The last enemy to be abolished is death' (I Cor. 15.26). Here is no pretence that death always comes as a gentle friend. Here death is not seen as the great deliverer from the 'tomb' or the 'dream' of this life. According to Plato's *Phaedo*, Socrates welcomed death. He forbade his disciples to express sorrow, and his last words were an instruction that as a sacrifice of thanksgiving for his death a cock should be offered to the god of healing. According to the New Testament, Jesus had a different attitude – one fully in accord with the Old Testament's horror of death. He expected his own death as a very great crisis. 'I have a baptism to undergo, and how hampered I am until the ordeal is over!' (Luke 12.50) He did not expect his followers to welcome death. 'Can you drink the cup that I am to drink?' (Matt. 20.22) He did not expect the families and friends of the dead to avoid grief; indeed, 'Jesus wept' (John 11.35). And when his own death drew near, he was anxious. 'Horror and dismay came over him, and he said to them, "My heart is ready to break with grief"' (Mark 14.34). 'His sweat was like clots of blood falling to the ground' (Luke 22.44). 'In the days of his earthly life he offered up prayers and petitions, with loud cries and tears, to God who was able to deliver him from the grave' (Heb. 5.7).

The writer to the Hebrews, who gave that reminder of Gethsemane, also recalled many who, 'through fear of death, had all their lifetime been in servitude' (Heb. 2.15). 'Miserable creature that I am,' wrote St Paul, 'who is there to rescue me out of this body doomed to death?' (Rom. 7.24) For years St Paul hoped that, now he was a Christian, he would not have to die. In an aside he remarked that some Christians who *had* died had done so because they had not received the Holy Communion properly (I Cor. 11.30). At the very least, the death of this body and the end of this age would test a person's spiritual life to the utmost, and in this crisis there was a terrible possibility of a spiritual catastrophe. This would be the great trial (*peirasmos*) of the end. That was what the Lord's Prayer originally meant in its petition that the disciple might be spared 'temptation'. That was what Jesus meant when he said to Peter, James and John in the Garden of Gethsemane: 'pray that you may be spared the test' (Mark 14.38).

Death, the enemy, is also an intruder into the Bible, which declares: man dies fearfully, but man is not meant to die. We cannot accept (or understand) everything in the Bible's link between death and Adam's sin; but we can now see that out of the experience to which the Bible bears witness, there emerges an inevitable conviction that death is not the proper end for the person whom God loves. And we who accept the inevitability of bodily deaths in the natural processes of the universe can pay a tribute to this great biblical protest against death. We can pay it the tribute of taking it seriously, although not literally. We can say that death is part of what we mean by 'sin' – if by 'sin' we mean all that is not fully worthy of the true dignity of man as a child of God.

3 *Eternal Death*

We can now see some meaning in the traditional pictures of hell. Hell is the alternative to being grasped and held by a power that is stronger than death. Hell is eternal death. And hell is possible because man's soul is *not* naturally immortal, whatever Plato said. In the second century, a theologian named Tatian gave the Christian reply to the Platonists. 'Of itself, the soul is not immortal, but mortal, O Greeks! Nevertheless, it is capable of not dying. If it does not know the truth, it dies and is dissolved with the body.'[3]

It has been traditional in Christian theology to draw a contrast between the 'pains of loss' (*poena damni*) and the pains experienced by one or other of the senses (*poena sensus*) in hell. But if we recognize that all descriptions of events in eternity are without exception myths, because they presuppose that time continues in eternity, then we can recognize that every pain of hell is a figment of the imagination, with the single and all-terrible exception of the pain of the loss of the life which comes from the loving power of God. We are delivered from innumerable nightmares – into the one fear that, while others are sustained through death by God, someone may not be. Someone may end in 'the punishment of eternal ruin, cut off from the presence of the Lord and the splendour of his might' (II Thess. 1.9). Someone may find that 'sin pays a wage, and the wage is death' (Rom. 6.23).

If no one escapes eternal death, then we can see that 'hell' is the fate of everyone, as the eternal half-life of Sheol or Hades was once believed to be the fate of all mankind. But if a single person in the whole of history has escaped this fate, then the questions of how and why any other person is judged worthy of hell become agonizing.

One error which the Bible did avoid was to say that anyone would be condemned to hell without deserving it. Always that fate was related to the absolute justice of God, and to the whole personality of the individual (to use a modern way of speaking). The possibility of an arbitrary or 'surprise' condemnation to hell, or the possibility of a person going to hell simply because he was predestined to it, should certainly never arise for us.

The Bible does, of course, contain many pictures of God as the final judge, or of Jesus Christ as exercising this power of final judgment on behalf of his Father. Behind such pictures is the Bible's conviction that all other claims to reality, truth or goodness are to be measured against the one reality, the truth and holiness of God. But the most mature insight of the Bible into the human condition does not see this judgment by God as something external to man. St John summed up all the tragedy of history in words of infinite sadness: 'the light has come into the world, but men preferred darkness to light because their deeds were evil' (John 3.19). The Jesus of St John is frequently described in that gospel as the judge of the world, as the one judge whose judgment is 'true' and 'just', but he is no external judge. 'If anyone hears my words and pays no regard to them, I am not his judge; I have not come to judge the world, but to save the world' (John 12.47). St John's idea that the word of Jesus will be a man's judge on the last day seems to involve the idea that the man who prefers his own lies to that truth, his own darkness to that light, has brought judgment on himself. If we may use modern expressions, we may say that this man has decided his own character, and thus his own destiny.

The Bible often teaches that no man makes this decision except in dialogue with God. He chooses – but God also chooses. This is what made St Augustine develop his doctrine of God's predestination of the 'elect' to eternal life. However, the Bible never says that God has forced anyone to do evil and has thus predestined that person to hell. Eleven centuries after St Augustine, John Calvin was driven by his lawyer's logic in the Reformation controversies (and by his failure to make Geneva a thoroughly well disciplined city of God) to emphasize the 'reprobation' of the damned who resisted the Gospel. His opponents' obstinacy could thus be interpreted as one more sign of the sovereignty of his God. God had made them like that. 'Whence does it happen that Adam's fall irremediably involved so many peoples, together with their infant offspring, in eternal death, unless it so pleased God?' Even Calvin immediately confessed that such a divine decree was 'dreadful indeed' (*horribile quidem*).[4] It is in fact an appallingly evil fantasy which has been renounced and denounced by the Arminians in the seventeenth century and by almost all modern theologians, including Calvin's theological heirs such as Karl Barth.

Predestination to hell can appeal to some words written by St Paul to the Romans, that God 'not only shows mercy as he chooses, but also makes men stubborn as he chooses. . . . What if God, desiring to exhibit his retribution at work and to make his power known, tolerated very patiently those vessels which were objects of retribution due for destruction, and did so in order to make known the full wealth of his splendour upon vessels which were objects of mercy, and which from the first had been prepared for this splendour?' (Rom. 9.18, 22, 23) An incidental speculation of this ambiguity should, however, be considered in its proper setting, which is the Bible's whole proclamation of 'God our Saviour, whose will it is that all men should find salvation and come to know the truth' (I Tim. 2.4). Even the grim reference to the 'eternal fire' adds that this fire is 'ready for the Devil and his angels', while the blessings of heaven have been ready for the righteous 'since the world was made' (Matt. 25.34, 41). St Paul himself hoped for 'acquittal and life for all men' (Rom. 5.18), and declared: 'In making all men prisoners to disobedience, God's purpose was to show mercy to all mankind' (Rom. 11.32). (This last text was a favourite with Karl Barth, who delighted to speak about Jesus Christ as the One in whom God declared his will to choose or 'elect' all men – a fascinating twist to the doctrine of predestination!)

As we have seen, the New Testament includes many passages which speak about the worst failure in belief or the worst failure in conduct as being incompatible with eternal life. The most fundamental of these passages is the warning by Jesus against slander of the Holy Spirit. That sin alone is 'beyond forgiveness' (Mark 3.28). It seems, therefore, that for the New Testament any profoundly serious failure in belief or conduct points to a failure to receive the Holy Spirit, and any completely disastrous failure is a failure to understand the Holy Spirit at all. All too many people who have heard or read the New Testament's warning against the unforgivable sin have tortured themselves with the possibility that they or those whom they love have been guilty of this sin. What exactly was this sin? Could someone commit it unintentionally? People have asked themselves such questions in curiosity, in fear, in great anguish and in madness.

The answer seems clear in the New Testament. It is the answer that 'slander of the Holy Spirit' means calling good (e.g. Jesus healing) evil (e.g. Satan at work). This sin is far worse than the sin of crucifying Jesus, for this sin is not one for which forgiveness can be asked because 'they do not know what they are doing' (Luke 23.34). This sin is the sin of people who *do* 'know' and are utterly wrong. It points to a total lack of understanding of truth or of goodness. It points to a nature entirely diseased and corrupt. And the New Testament is stating no more than what is obvious when it says that a person who had no understanding of truth or goodness, who was evil throughout, could not enter into fellowship with the one true God who is holy. Such a person would have no capacity at all to enable him to enter such a fellowship. More: he would not have the slightest wish to do so. He could not be forgiven, because he could not accept forgiveness. A person in such a condition would have made himself into the garbage of humanity. The Bible's comparisons of that condition with Jerusalem's incinerator need not be treated like photographs of hell if we are to see their main purpose, which was to express the idea of utter degradation.

The Bible repeatedly warns that it *is* possible for a man to reach that condition of calling good evil and degrading all life including his own. Optimists in the history of Christianity, taking a liberally benevolent view of human nature, have repeatedly rejected such warnings. Origen at the end of the third century seems to have believed that at the end all souls, and even the Devil and his angels, must be saved. Perhaps he merely hoped that this would be so –

75

his language is confused. But it is clear that in this respect his thought was essentially Platonic, not biblical. He believed also in the pre-existence of souls – a soul which had been created some time earlier assumed a body; and he affirmed that, by purification after the death of every body, every soul would eventually be restored to its original purity.

This doctrine was condemned by orthodox Catholics as being contrary to the Bible's warnings about hell, and Gregory of Nyssa in the fourth century was the only theologian of importance who shared Origen's hope. The belief that salvation would eventually be universal, for all men ('universalism'), was revived in the sixteenth century by groups on the fringes of the Protestant Reformation, the Anabaptists and the Socinians. The group known as the Cambridge Platonists maintained it in the seventeenth century. The belief that all would be saved became popular among many Protestants during the course of the nineteenth century, under the influence of the two greatest theologians of the century, Friedrich Schleiermacher and F. D. Maurice. In England controversies arose around expressions of hope by a contributor to the volume called *Essays and Reviews* and by a popular preacher, F. W. Farrar. In 1864 the Privy Council gave much offence to the orthodox by refusing to condemn as illegal 'the expression of hope by a clergyman that even the ultimate pardon of the wicked, who are condemned in the day of judgment, may be consistent with the will of God'. It was said that this legal verdict had taken away the Englishman's last hope of everlasting damnation. Among the non-Fundamentalist Protestants of the United States, many preachers abandoned 'hell-fire' preaching and nursed instead what was called 'the larger hope'. Universalism, often freed from the hesitations which clouded the nineteenth-century theologians, enjoys widespread popularity in our own day.

But are optimists right to be unhesitant? A great trouble about some statements of universalism is that they fail to do justice to the reality and depth of human evil. Some of the theologians who have taught belief in the salvation of all have made this part of a doctrinal system which owes more to the optimism of some philosophical fashion of the day – Platonism, for example, or Victorian liberalism – than it does to the Bible. The Bible repeatedly stresses the evil ingrained in the human heart. The murderer is among the sons of Adam, the traitor is among the disciples of Jesus, the chief of sinners is in every man. The Bible is mythological in saying how this evil got there (Adam's fall) – but not in saying that it *is* there. The Bible is mythological in depicting the Devil and his angels, the little demons – but not in saying that what is good in man confronts an opposition which often wins ('Satan' comes from the Hebrew for 'the Adversary').[5] And this unflattering portrait of man is believable now, in a century when man has so often shown himself to be his own worst enemy. In our age of many tragedies, we are reasonable if we prefer the biblical realism to all secular sentimentalities.

The Bible's vision of life, for all its sense of tragedy, is – let us say it again – dominated by a grateful praise of the loving power of God and by a triumphant faith that God's kingship will be obeyed. The great city of Nineveh will be converted, says that delightful short story, the Book of Jonah; the lost coin, the lost sheep, the lost son will be found. St Paul and St John, two of the most eloquent commentators on the evil in the world, saw the consequences of that vision when they prophesied that all men would be drawn to Christ and 'all things' reconciled to God through him. Origen, Maurice, Schleiermacher, Barth – what a row of theological giants! – and all the universalists have been in very good company in believing that this is the purpose of God. They have also been thoroughly in accordance with hopes expressed in the New Testament itself when they have hoped that after death God's goodness, as declared in Christ, will appeal to those who did not accept the Gospel of Christ while alive on earth. In the New Testament as well as in these universalist theologians, the hope is clear and strong that this activity of God's goodness after death will so heal mankind that all human life becomes the Church triumphant. Outside the Church there will be no salvation – and the hope is that there will be no one outside the Church. St John the Divine, in his vision of the final City of God, saw two trees of life. 'The leaves of the trees serve for the healing of the nations, and every accursed thing shall disappear' (Rev. 22.2).

But the Bible does *not* say that the healing of the nations is *bound* to include everyone. If universalists do say this, then they defy the Bible. They defy not only the many biblical passages which threaten sinners with the divine wrath, but also the Bible's deepest insight – the insight that if men resist God's love, the only weapon which God uses is the weapon of the cross. The cross is the appeal to the conscience of a love which suffers. God will not have men's enforced obedience. He has chosen to create men who are free to choose in dialogue with him. If after all the dialogue they choose against him, he does not then cease to respect their freedom. This is the Bible's most breathtaking extreme of humanism: its acceptance of the freedom of the will. Man may reject the goodness of God and prefer evil, reject eternal life and prefer death. And God, who created man, who loves man, will not make man say 'yes'. According to the Bible, God may take man's 'no' for an answer.

Will any person make that choice and persevere in it to the end, so that his life becomes incompatible with the life of God? The Bible cannot say, for the end has not yet come. There is a great tension in the Bible, emphasizing with all possible vigour the radical seriousness of those choices in belief and conduct which decide character and destiny. And we shall be wise not to say either, until we join the praise of the victorious God by 'every created thing' (Rev. 5.13).

4 *The Real Meaning of Resurrection*

But if the meaning of hell is eternal death, what is the

meaning for us of the biblical symbol of the resurrection to eternal life?

We cannot take seriously the picture of harps above the clouds or the picture of revived corpses on earth. Theoretically it is conceivable that God, if he has the power attributed to him in the Bible, will choose to arrange an incessant concert in heaven or the evacuation of the world's graveyards. In practice these images of 'the world to come' have gone dead on modern men, who realize (more vividly perhaps than all the generations did before the age of science) just how miraculous celestial harps or revived corpses would be – and who find themselves without any wish for such miracles to happen. St John the Divine (Rev. 4.1–5.8) pictured the Lamb standing on a throne, with seven horns, seven eyes and the capacity to handle a scroll and break its seven seals. 'One whose appearance was like the gleam of jasper and cornelian' sat on this throne. Four creatures, each with six wings and 'eyes all over', guarded it. Around it were twenty-four elders, each sitting on his own throne and armed with a harp, a golden bowl full of incense and a crown which was laid before the throne continuously. The other traditional picture, of all the dead assembled in their bodies for judgment just outside Jerusalem, seems even more ridiculously over-crowded. It is clear to almost everyone that these pictures cannot be taken literally and cannot be kept as the main images of eternity.

In this psychological situation, the question must be faced whether it is wise for the Christian Church to retain in its creed belief in 'the resurrection of the flesh' or in 'the resurrection of the body'. It can be claimed that the second of these phrases is compatible with St Paul's warning that 'flesh and blood can never possess the kingdom of God' (I Cor. 15.50), for 'the body' in eternity will be a 'spiritual body'. However, the original intention of the Apostles' Creed to teach the resurrection of the flesh, contradicting St Paul, is clear. The Latin and Greek versions made it clear originally, and many translations into modern language have kept it clear. Luther substituted 'the body' for 'the flesh' in the sixteenth century and the English Prayer Book followed, but there was no intention of making a basic change (the Prayer Book kept 'the flesh' in the Baptism services). In the seventeenth century the Roman Catholic Church's Council of Trent and the (Presbyterian) Westminster Confession both echoed the faith of Tertullian fifteen centuries before that 'all of the body, in every man, the identical body, the entire body' would be raised.[6]

Belief in the resurrection of the flesh has been defended by some conservative theologians within the twentieth century, but almost everyone now regards it as a ludicrous error, and the churches' approval of cremation is one small sign of this. It is very doubtful whether 'the resurrection of the body' is a good alternative. The distinction between 'the flesh' and 'the body' is a very difficult idea which is probably unintelligible to the vast majority of people. If what is meant here by 'the body' is in fact 'the person', why not say so? Why not be more honest in translating or revising the original idea of the resurrection of the flesh? Or why not use the simpler phrase of the Nicene Creed, 'the resurrection of the dead'?

When the Apostles' Creed was first compiled, the modern word 'personality' was not known. But now that this word exists and is widely understood, the continued use of the ancient Roman phrase which is so open to criticism or laughter cannot be justified except on grounds of diplomacy rather than theology. And what are the grounds of diplomacy? The problem is how to avoid further divisions between Christians caused by the apparently arrogant action of one church or group of churches producing a new creed. The solution of this problem surely lies in trying to reach agreement on an ecumenical creed by discussion among Christians.

The replacement of the Apostles' Creed in the life of the Christian Church is obviously a matter of much gravity and delicacy. But we may be bolder to undertake the necessary work if we acknowledge fully two truths about this creed.

In the first place, it was not compiled by the apostles. The English version now in common use was based on the Latin version used in the late Middle Ages. With minor variations, this creed goes back to a creed which was developed in Rome for teaching candidates for baptism probably about AD 150.[7]

In the second place, other parts of the so-called Apostles' Creed seem to need revision, so that a modern discussion among Christians could have a comprehensive aim. One phrase requiring attention in English is 'He descended into hell' – in Latin, 'He descended to the lower regions' (descendit ad inferna). Some modern Prayer Books add a footnote explaining that the word 'hell' or inferna means 'the abode of the dead', but it scarcely helps us to think that the goal of Christ's visit was Sheol not Gehenna. The phrase rests on ambiguous New Testament passages and comes dangerously near to identifying Christianity with the 'three-decker' view of the universe (with heaven above and hell beneath the earth). It does little to help us to imagine for ourselves the meaning of this myth of 'the harrowing of hell': the victory of God as embracing all men and all things in all ages, the victory which is a universe wider than the other 'Catholic' picture of salvation as confined to 'all saints' or to 'all souls of the faithful departed'. When the Apostles' Creed is sung, the music is not triumphant here, and perhaps most worshippers have never realized that this phrase is a triumphant Gospel for the whole human race.

Many of the traditional symbols of God's victory and eternal life will, no doubt, continue to be used in the worship and thought of Christians, but this does not seem to justify the present widespread attitude that the Church should never consider the adoption of a new ecumenical creed which attempts to be a short summary of the things which every Christian believes. Nor should the continuance of the biblical pictures and the great medieval hymns ('Jerusalem the golden', 'O what their joy and their glory must be') mean that present-day Christians should believe that eternal life means the continuance of this life lived in the flesh. Many traditional prayers convey a false impression of what a modern Christian believes by their references to eternal life as being 'throughout all ages, world without end'. The Christian today, if he considers his faith intelligently, cannot hold that eternal life will consist of a number of periods of history. Nor can he hold that it will consist of the life of this world going on for ever. No! Time must have a stop. The world must have an end.

The biblical symbol of the resurrection of the body can, however, have a place in a modern Christian's belief if this symbol stands for the faith that *the whole of history is taken into the life of God.* This includes the whole of my history, from the moment of my conception to the moment of my death. It includes the history of the whole human race, from the moment when *homo erectus* could be distinguished from a man-like animal (a moment known only to God) to the moment when the last man dies in fire or cold or disease or old age. Many would say that the whole of life is also included – the animals, the fish, the birds, the insects, all living creatures. Many would add, too, that the whole of the creation is included, for no sharp break comes between life and matter. 'All things are included', as St Paul said, expanding the biblical image of the new earth in the coming age of the resurrection.

Whether or not we include the animal kingdom or the lifeless creation in the meaning of the symbol of resurrection, we can all agree that the whole of the life which must be included has had a physical basis. 'Man is what he eats,' said a nineteenth-century atheist. He was exaggerating. But it is true that in this life man cannot live without bread, nor mind without matter. In the Middle Ages St Thomas Aquinas wisely taught that nothing is present in the intellect which has not first been present in the senses – and it was this belief, derived from Aristotle, that made St Thomas think the 'resurrection of the body' necessary. The man who is 'raised' is not only a spiritual being, but is also a child, a consumer and a citizen, whose belief and conduct, character and destiny, have been shaped by influences which may be examined by doctors, economists and students of the hard facts of politics. Man may be 'lower than the angels' or 'a little less than God' (Ps. 8.5), but he is also an animal whose nature may be analysed by biochemists, biologists and anthropologists. Eternity is not reserved for souls who are glad to escape from this world, regarding it as a world of shadows or distractions. Eternity is for creatures made in, and partially by, this world.

A brief excursion into biblical psychology may be suggestive here. In the Bible, the flesh (*basar* in Hebrew and *sarx* in Greek) is given life by its soul (*nephesh* in Hebrew and *psyche* in Greek). The soul was like a man's breath, and when his breath left his flesh, that flesh returned to the dust from which Adam had been made (e.g. Ps. 146.4). But there was in man also a spirit (*ruach* in Hebrew and *pneuma* in Greek). This was not the mere breath of life, but was like the mighty desert wind. (*Ruach* was the Hebrew word for the wind.) It came and it went while a man still had his soul. 'Soul' and 'spirit' could be used interchangeably, but St Paul brought out the difference when he described human nature as 'spirit, soul and body' (I Thess. 5.23). The writer to the Hebrews also thought that the soul could be divided from the spirit (Heb. 4.12). St Paul's hope of resurrection was not that the *sarx* would be raised, or that the *psyche* would be immortal. It was a hope that the body would cease to be animated by the mere breath of life (what St Paul called *soma psychikon*) and would become an instrument of the great Spirit (*soma pneumatikon*). 'If there is such a thing as an animal body, there is also a spiritual body' (I Cor. 15.44), or a body like that of 'the heavenly man' (I Cor. 15.49), or a liberated body (Rom. 8.23).

This was the hope that led St Paul to his great vision of the whole of creation as involved in the hope of the resurrection or Spiritualization of the body. 'For the created universe waits with eager expectation for God's sons to be revealed. . . . The universe itself is to be freed from the shackles of mortality and enter upon the liberty and splendour of the children of God' (Rom. 8.19, 21). Whatever may be the truth for us in that mystical vision of nature, we can understand more of the biblical teaching that until history comes to this glorious end each individual is somehow incomplete and impatient. In St John the Divine's vision, the Christian martyrs give a great cry: 'How long, sovereign Lord, holy and true, must it be before thou wilt vindicate us . . .?' (Rev. 6.10). In St Paul's vision, all Christians join a quieter cry. 'Even we, to whom the Spirit is given as firstfruits of the harvest to come, are groaning inwardly while we wait for God to make us his sons' – or rather, to make it clear that we were his sons from the beginning (Rom. 8.23). The vindication of God must involve that completion of the purpose of God in history. The individual who is 'raised' must await that social and cosmic 'resurrection'.

The promise of 'resurrection' comes, therefore, to creatures who belong to the universe whose 'groans as if in pangs of childbirth' were heard by St Paul (Rom. 8.22). It is a promise that their future will be not less but *more* lively and happy than their past. However, the transition from time to eternity is not made smoothly. The biblical symbol of 'resurrection' stands also for the reality of death. All this history ends. All nature decays and is changed. 'Everything the world affords, all that panders to the appetites, or entices the eyes, all the glamour of its life . . . is passing away with all its allurements' (I John 2.16, 17). But not only *that* world dies. The best dies. All of everything and everyone dies. One phrase in the Apostles' Creed which we can take literally is 'Was crucified, dead and buried'. 'Resurrection' is a symbol of the faith that what really was dead can really be given a new life.

5 *Conditions of Eternity*

Rupert Brooke believed that the conventional idea of heaven could be parodied thus:

> But somewhere, beyond Space and Time,
> Is wetter water, slimier slime . . .
> And in that Heaven of all their wish
> There shall be no more land, say fish.

And some of St Augustine's speculations about the resurrection of the flesh justify such a parody. But there is in the Christian tradition a purer stream, and we can see it in St Augustine's own golden sentence about the heavenly life: 'There we shall rest, and we shall see; we shall see, and we shall love; we shall love, and we shall praise.'[8] Such words reflect the experience of contemplation in Christian prayer as well as the purification of the Greek philosopher's intellectual desire. Indeed, they echo the New Testament, for our little jokes about harps and hymns do not do justice to the New Testament's central message, which is that to praise God is to exist according to his will. This is not an unending flattery of God. It is a completely loving adjustment to God, whose will is done perfectly.

Such a prospect contains no trace of boredom. The Bible associates the idea of God with the happiest experiences of a man's life – with peace and security, with vigour and victory, with deliverance and all that is beautiful, with a marriage and a feast; and again and again the Bible repeats or implies that to know God, to see God, to obey God, to live in his presence, is 'fullness of joy' (Ps. 16.11). In the twentieth century, Christian faith has grown so preoccupied with its problems and duties that it has largely forgotten that happiness lies at the heart of its good news, in the secret foundation of its fellowship, and at the end of its promise. Reversing the emphasis in their Lord's own teaching, Christians think of their lives as battles not banquets. It may be that no greater contribution can be made to the reform and restatement of Christianity in our time than to make its joy more obvious; for only after seeing the happiness of God's worshippers on earth can people be persuaded that the prospect of 'praising' God for ever is attractive.

But 'we shall rest'? Heaven surely contains no trace of

selfish idleness. People who know from their own bitter experience how absorption in the self is hell on earth, and how boredom grows like a poisonous plant in empty soil, dread the prospect of an idle eternity. But the New Testament speaks of the blessedness of the dead in terms of corporate activity. 'Rest in peace!' is the hope of a pagan who dreads the return of his dead. The Christian hope is, rather, that the dead 'may rest from their labours' (Rev. 14.13) – from all their toil, on earth, with the pains and frustrations involved in earthly work. The Bible has a healthy realism in its acknowledgment of the fact that work is not fun for most people most of the time, and here the Bible is to be preferred to the modern 'Gospel of work' which sentimentally supposes that the moments of joy which many workers know (particularly writers such as those who write about the Gospel of work) are typical of work as a whole.

We may add that the work which the Bible pictures as going on in heaven is the praise of God for what he is and does. In other words, it is adjustment to the work of God. Despite the Jewish belief that God began resting on the seventh day of creation, Jesus was regarded as having revealed that 'my Father has never yet ceased his work' (John 5.17). The comparison of the dead with 'the angels' may be instructive in this connection. The angels were mythological figures, and most of them were imported into the Old Testament world from Persia. (Zoroastrianism was strong on angelology as well as on the resurrection of the body.) But *angelos* was Greek for 'messenger', and the basic idea was simply that of God acting; the Archangel Gabriel was God's message to Mary in Nazareth. It may be legitimate for us to think of the dead as being adjusted to God's action, God's work, so that they become parts of it, and this may be the truth in the traditional picture of the saints as being patrons of causes and people on earth.

But if the Bible corrects many modern fears about the flattery, the boredom and the idleness in heaven, it also corrects many sentimental hopes. For example, there is no emphasis in the New Testament on the reunions of families or friends in heaven. Indeed, Jesus himself was recorded as having taught that 'when they rise from the dead, men and women do not marry' and meant (as the story around this saying shows) 'do not remain married' (Mark 12.25).

This seems a hard saying for widows or widowers. The story implies, however, some continuance of the family, for it says that God wills to be the God of Abraham, his son and grandson. The meaning seems to be that while the formation of character and destiny by family life will endure, there will be no *exclusive* relationships in eternal life, for all will be perfectly one with all. The unity which a husband and wife have begun to experience in the best moments of their marriage is to be the reality enjoyed by all, for all will be united with God who is the source of their being. The New Testament prefers to speak of a congregation, not a marriage, as being the best foretaste of heaven, because a congregation is more inclusive and is more clearly based on the worship of God. Here lies the Christian's best assurance that even before death he has glimpsed the unity of 'the full concourse and assembly of the first-born citizens of heaven, and God the judge of all, and the spirits of good men made perfect' (Heb. 12.24).

The New Testament is also against the popular idea that the dead, if they survive at all, are made perfect without any trouble. 'Paradise' is promised to a man who, while they are both being tortured to death, expects Jesus to show himself as king (Luke 23.43); heaven is seen by the first martyr, who is being stoned to death (Acts 7.56); eternal life is expected by St Paul and experienced here and now by St John – but beside these passages must be set the references to the dead, even to the Christian dead, as 'sleeping' (I Cor. 15.6, 20; I Thess. 4.14, 15; II Peter 3.4). Such references might not mean much, for the comparison of death with sleep is age-old; thus it is said that a little dead girl is really sleeping (Mark 5.39), and that the martyred St Stephen 'fell asleep' (Acts 7.60). However, with the idea of sleeping goes the idea of renewal. In St John the Divine's vision, the dead are awakened and washed before they join the praise of God. Jesus is said to have warned his hearers that some would need to be disciplined, as in his symbolic sayings about severe and less severe floggings (Luke 12.48) and about paying the last farthing before release (Matt. 5.26). Here is the basis of the Roman Catholic Church's idea of Purgatory, an idea corrupted by the crude notion of days or years of punishment.

Such symbols represent the profound conviction that 'it is a terrible thing to fall into the hands of the living God' (Heb. 10.31). The adjustment to God in eternity must be terrible because of the contrast between our life and God's, our sin and his holiness, our time and his eternity. Yet in the end God's eternity witnesses the triumph of God's holiness, so that sinful men become 'like angels' – or 'like him' (John 3.2).

6 *God's Memory of Us*

The New Testament confesses its almost complete agnosticism about the nature of that eternal life, 'that age'. 'Here and now, dear friends, we are God's children; what we shall be has not yet been disclosed' (I John 3.2). What it does say about eternity is based on earthly experience. St John in this very passage declares that 'we shall be like him, *because* we shall see him as he is'; in other words, the earthly experience of a brief and clouded vision of God has already purified Christians – how much more will the vision of God 'face to face' (I Cor. 13.12)! Indeed, the whole idea of God and his 'coming age' as being infinitely long, everlasting or timeless is based on the experience of moments when time seems to stand still and when life is intense, glorious and friendly, as in St Paul's vision of Paradise (II Cor. 12.1–6). If those moments seemed eternal, how much more must the life of God transcend all the limitations of life on earth!

Eternal life is for the New Testament the divine life. God alone does not depend on a body. 'God in eternal felicity alone holds sway. He is King of kings and Lord of lords; he alone possesses immortality, dwelling in unapproachable light' (I Tim. 6.15, 16). The eternal hope of man is derived from this. In this life we owe our existence, and all creation owes its being, entirely to the one Creator – how much more must eternal life have that one source! 'After this life,' said St Augustine in his exposition of Psalm 30, 'God himself will be our place.' The New Testament makes the same affirmation. 'His divine power has bestowed on us everything that makes for life and true religion, enabling us to know the One who called us by his own splendour and might. Through this might and splendour he has given us his promises, great beyond all price, and through them you may escape the corruption with which lust has infected the world, and come to share the very being of God' (II Peter 1.3, 4).

This insight into man's eternal 'place' in God comes dangerously near to obscuring the distinction between the Creator and the creature – the distinction which the whole Bible stresses with great passion. The classic Hindu belief is that the individual and the eternal One are already essentially united, as salt and water are united in salt water; the *Atman*, deep down, is the *Brahman*. The classic Hindu hope is, therefore, that the individual will see his own eternal foundation – and, seeing that, will fully *be* eternal, as a drop of water enters the ocean. The problem for a restatement of the faith of the New Testament is how to combine the hope of sharing the very being of God with the need to remain for ever distinct from that being, as a fish in the ocean remains the fish it was up the river.[9]

One clue may be found in the conception of eternal life as *God's memory of us*. Every man is aware of the importance of memories in his life. His basic equipment – genetic, as science now shows – existed before any memory. But his memories make up much of what makes him a man; they record the events which constitute the pattern into which new events are fitted and become personal for him. In every man's experience of his own past may be found a hint of what the union of God with his creatures may mean eternally. God is before any creature was; and men can glimpse the truth that God could exist without them. But the taking of God's creation into eternal life enriches him; and men can glimpse the love of his creation which lies at the heart of God's creativity.

When a man remembers, he is not merely a blank sheet on which a past event is printed. He interprets as he remembers. He sees the significance of the past. He can see its evil significance, but often the memory buries what was unpleasant or wrong. It can go to hell! And often our memories transfigure and glorify what was good in the past. A day of happiness is given a greater joy as it is remembered, and a thing of beauty is seen in a radiant splendour which originally was not seen. Here, too, in ordinary human experience there may be a foretaste of the destruction of what was wrong and the glory of what was good in creation.

A great deal in the science of psychology is built on the capacity of men to remember. Men can remember far more than they expect. They can remember much, or all, of what they *want* to remember. Freud showed this in developing psychoanalysis, but those who reject Freudian theories can and do accept the discovery of the astonishing power of the human memory. This may be a clue to the power of God to hold his creation in eternal life. From our own experience of our memories we can go on to glimpse God's will and capacity to remember for ever the whole of creation, each moment of life in it, so that the life of God completely counteracts what the philosopher A. N. Whitehead used to call 'the 'perishing of occasions'. And more: since God loves people and things more than mere 'occasions', he remembers completely that person or that thing as that person or thing was shaped in the whole of life before death. But even here the comparison of the human and divine memories cannot be ended. When we remember, the person remembered can 'come alive', as we say, for a moment of illusion. A period of history can be 'recreated' in a book of history. And this, the most impressive aspect of the power of our memories and the summit of all historical work, can be a clue to the will of God to remain the God of Abraham, Isaac and Jacob, and the God of every living creature, rescuing all that has existed from the 'hell' of eternal death.

'May he remember all your offerings!' was the psalmist's prayer for his king (Ps. 20.3). 'Remember, O Lord, in David's favour all the hardships which he endured!' (Ps. 132.1). 'Remember not the sins of my youth, or my transgressions!' was the psalmist's prayer for himself (Ps. 25.7). 'Remember me, O Lord, when thou showest favour to thy people!' (Ps. 106.4). Such simple prayers show how ancient, and how natural, is the comparison between the human and divine memories which we have just made in outline. In the Old Testament, God's remembrance of the dead was a prospect which could arouse no enthusiasm. But the New Testament shows that the life and death of Jesus made the great difference, and in the New Testament when the first man begins to see what kind of destiny is revealed on the cross of Jesus, he says: 'Jesus, remember me when you come to your throne!' (Luke 23.43).

NOTES

1. Walther Eichrodt, *Theology of the Old Testament*, vol. ii, London: SCM Press and Philadelphia: Westminster Press, 1968, p. 525.

2. Martin Noth, *Exodus*, London: SCM Press and Philadelphia: Westminster Press, 1962, p. 45.

3. Jaroslav Pellkan, *The Shape of Death*, New York: Macmillan, 1962, p. 17. It is curious to observe how in the nineteenth century when Mr Gladstone found himself driven to a similar conclusion, his orthodoxy was suspected by his fellow-churchmen. In his *The Household of Faith* (London: Mowbray, 1906), G. W. E. Russell recalled Gladstone in his old age. 'In August, 1895, it was my privilege to spend a week at Hawarden . . . Never shall I forget the hour when I sat with him in the park, while a thunderstorm was gathering over our heads, and he, all unheeding, poured forth, in those organ-notes of profound conviction, his belief that the human soul is not necessarily indestructible, but that Immortality is the gift of God in Christ to the believer. The impression of that discourse will not be effaced until the tablets of

memory are finally blotted.' But when Gladstone wrote of this conviction in his *Studies Subsidiary to the Works of Bishop Butler*, he preferred to think of 'the righteous', rather than 'the believer', as the recipient of immortality.

4. *Institutes of the Christian Religion*, 33.7. See François Wendel, *Calvin*, Fontana paperback, 1965.

5. For the life of Satan, see Giovanni Papini, *The Devil*, London: Eyre and Spottiswoode, 1955 and New York: E. P. Dutton & Co., 1954.

6. *De Resurrectione Carnis* (63), a disastrously influential work. The best presentation of 'Immortality and Resurrection in the Philosophy of the Church Fathers' is in the Ingersoll Lecture by H. A. Wolfson, reprinted in *Immortality and Resurrection*, ed. Krister Stendahl, New York: Macmillan, 1965.

7. This Roman creed was quoted by a bishop, Marcellus, in 340 and by a theologian, Tyrannius Rufinus, about 404. Incidentally the creed as quoted by Marcellus included the final phrase 'And the life eternal' (*zoen aionion*), but Rufinus stopped short at 'the resurrection of the flesh'. The shorter version quoted by Rufinus was the earlier version, and a few years later St Augustine, in the ninth of his sermons to catechumens, explained why the addition had been made. It was to assure believers that the flesh in which they would arise would last for ever. It would resemble the flesh of the risen Christ, not the flesh of Lazarus who had certainly been raised but who had presumably died again.

8. *City of God*, 30.

9. Recent discussion by theologians who use the 'Process' philosophy of A. N. Whitehead include the essays published by Schubert Ogden in *The Reality of God*, London: SCM Press and New York: Harper & Row, 1967, pp. 206–230, and by Peter Hamilton in *The Living God and the Modern World*, London: Hodder and Stoughton, 1967, pp. 108–141. Such writers stress the 'objective immortality' of God. Hamilton sums it up: 'Everything of any value in our life will be . . . immortalized in his supremely personal life'. He quotes Charles Hartshorne, another Process philosopher, on the religious strength of this hope: 'Not *our* personality is this necessary, this primary, personal unity, but only God's. It is a hard lesson to learn – that God is more important than we are.' However, in my own exposition I include also a version of the hope of 'personal' or 'subjective' survival, described by Hartshorne as 'the common notion of immortality, that after death we begin a new series of adventures bound together by a prolongation of our present personality'. This hope is derived from the biblical revelation that the Creator loves persons, and thinks them important eternally.

4 The Rising Man

1 *The Meaning of History*

It has often been alleged that the Christian vision of eternity amounts to 'pie in the sky when I die' (a phrase which comes from an Australian song). The last chapter was intended to show that any attack on the Christian vision as being selfish or materialistic is unfair. But we have now to face the charge that the Christian vision is escapist. Many in this age of Marx and Freud believe that it is. They allege that all religion, but particularly the religion patronized by the European and North American upper and middle classes, is 'opium for the people'. In the nineteenth century a horse or other beast of burden might be given a small dose of opium to keep it quiet while its burdens were being put on it, and the allegation is that the hope of heaven is used to keep the poor quiet while they are being exploited. Or more subtly, belief in the heavenly Father may be attacked as a neurotic illusion, by which weak and sick minds seek a compensation for unsatisfactory relationships with fathers and others on earth.

Religion has very often been misused like that, and of course the Bible itself can be made to support such attitudes. But the Bible is about kings, farmers and mothers, about the earth, flesh and blood, about sex and hatred. An instrument of torture is driven into its heart. The men and women in the pages of the Bible find themselves in turbulent conversation not only with each other but also with a God who is no pink cloud but a king with painfully definite commands and plans. And out of this experience on the earth there emerges something which is the very opposite of escapist literature, and which is in fact rather close to the purpose behind the work of those prophets of Israel, Karl Marx and Sigmund Freud. It is nothing less than a vision of the whole of history.

An interpretation of history is both visionary and intensely practical. It shows what a man thinks are the most important things in the world around him – and it does more. By placing all other things under those chosen things, and by saying that all other things acquire their meaning from their relationship with those chosen things, it is really a demand that everyone else should in practice prefer those things to all other things. It is not only a vision of the past; it is also a call to action. It not only views the world; it also changes it.

Thus a patriotic poet or historian, by recounting the deeds that freed the nation or won its empire or inspired its culture or built its prosperity, is really summoning his readers to serve the cause of the nation. A writer who sees history as the slow victory of reason over barbarism, as many historians did in the eighteenth century, is really advising us to be more proud of being reasonable. On 15 October 1764, Edward Gibbon 'sat musing amidst the ruins of the Capitol' during his first visit to Rome. Around him lay evidence of the triumph of religious superstition over a great, and on the whole a happy, civilization. As Gibbon's autobiography recalled, it was while 'the barefooted fryars were singing Vespers in the Temple of Jupiter, that the idea of writing the decline and fall of the City first started to my mind'. On the other hand, Freud's vision in his book on *Civilization and its Discontents* was of a 'reasonable' civilization which had repressed the instincts and energies of human nature, with the result that human nature had smouldered in discontents and erupted in violence. Freud urged on us a greater understanding of the emotions, a greater compassion, a more wholehearted acceptance of life – just as Gibbon urged us to prefer reason to religion.[1]

A man who writes a great history of inventions is really offering us a vision of man as the tool-maker (*homo faber*), and he hopes that we shall put our effort or support behind the advance of technology. A political thinker such as Karl Marx, who considers economic factors to be the most important in determining the course of history, writes his immense *Capital* as well as the *Communist Manifesto* in order to urge us to be on the right side in the class war. A more liberal historian, who sees history as the story of liberty and of man's sacrifices for it, is really urging us to defend freedom. In the nineteenth century the great British historian and commentator on society, Lord Acton, collected a large library in order to write a history of liberty. That book was never written, but the library survives, as does Lord Bryce's memory of how

> twenty years ago, late at night, in his library at Cannes, he expounded to me his views of how such a history of liberty might be written, and how it might be made the central thread of all history. He spoke for six or seven minutes only; but he spoke like a man inspired . . . The eloquence was splendid; but greater than the eloquence was the penetrating vision which discerned through all events and in all ages the play of those moral forces, now creating, now destroying, always transmuting, which had moulded and remoulded human institutions, and had given to the human spirit its ceaselessly changing forms of energy. It was as if the whole landscape of history had been suddenly lit up by a burst of sunlight.[2]

Like Gibbon or Freud, Marx or Acton, Jesus also had a vision of history. He was not one of those far more numerous religious teachers who have believed that history is unreal, or does not matter, or does not matter except as a return to a golden age in the past or to a static perfection in nature.[3] Jesus was a Jew, the heir of all the Old Testament's insistence that history is a real, important drama which moves towards an end controlled by God. Jesus saw history as the coming of the kingdom of God. And either he or his early followers worked out a sweeping reinterpretation of all the history which they knew.

St Luke indicates this. He gives us the story of how Jesus on the road to Emmaus 'explained to them the passages which referred to himself in every part of the scriptures', and the disciples felt their hearts on fire (Luke 24.25–32). St Luke also presents the first Christian sermon (St Peter's on the first Whitsunday) as an interpretation of the Old Testament, and the first Christian theology as St Stephen's long account of the true meaning of the days of Abraham and Moses (Acts 2.14–36, 7.2–53). It has been stressed in recent study of the gospels how St Luke, in particular, saw Jesus in the middle of time. That was why, beginning his story, he listed not only the ancestors of Jesus but also the political and religious rulers of the age, and why his two volumes moved from the temple at Jerusalem to the streets of Rome, the capital of the world. St Luke may have gained this world-embracing vision from St Paul, who has left us his own theology of history, written for the Romans. He may also have developed insights which had their origin in the teaching of the historical Jesus, and which are also reflected in the other surviving gospels.

The gospel written in Rome by St Mark implies a whole interpretation of the literature and history of Israel when it quotes the voice sounding in the ears of Jesus at his baptism: 'Thou art my Son, my Beloved; on thee my favour rests' (Mark 1.11). The voice here quotes, and unites, two very different phrases from the Old Testament. The first is a decree which God was believed to have issued in defence of a king of Israel: 'You are my son' (Ps. 2.7). This passage continues: 'Ask of me, and I will make the nations your heritage. . . . You shall break them with a rod of iron.' The other phrase seems to echo a song about an unknown political prisoner in an hour of defeat and exile: 'Behold my servant, whom I uphold, my chosen in whom my soul delights' (Isa. 42.1). This passage continues: 'He will bring forth justice to the nations . . . He will not cry nor lift up his voice . . . a bruised reed he will not break.' St Mark has scarcely written 150 words before he implies that 'Jesus Christ the Son of God' will be a Messiah who will exercise his kingship over the nations by wielding justice quietly and tenderly. This is the king who, although crucified, will to the end 'go on before you into Galilee and you will see him there' (Mark 16.7) – into Galilee, that mixture of the peoples from many nations.

The Jesus whom St Mark proclaims in his gospel, for a church facing martyrdom, is a Jesus who is confident of his power over the demons of disease and over the storms of nature. He is also a Jesus who believes that he will rise triumphant over the tragedy which will come through the demons and storms of human evil. St Mark tells us that the crucial moment at the trial of Jesus was when Jesus admitted to the high priest that he did claim to be 'the Messiah, the Son of the Blessed One'. At that moment Jesus adds: 'and you will see the Son of Man seated on the right hand of God and coming with the clouds of heaven' (Mark 14.61, 62).

This is a claim that his quiet, tender kingship, now doomed to death, will be vindicated in the 'coming age'. It is a quotation from the Book of Daniel's account of visions 'by night' of evil empires. These empires appear in the form of a lion (Babylon), a bear (the Medes), a leopard (the Persians) and a beast with great iron teeth (Alexander the Great and his heirs). Here is a short history of the world. Then God, 'the Ancient of Days', takes his seat on his throne to judge all this history . . .

> and behold, with the clouds of heaven
>   there came one like a son of man,
> and he came to the Ancient of Days
>   and was presented before him.
>
> And to him was given dominion
>   and glory and kingdom,
> that all peoples, nations and languages
>   should serve him.
>
> His dominion is an everlasting dominion,
>   which shall not pass away,
> and his Kingdom one
>   that shall not be destroyed. (Dan. 7.13, 14)

This man, coming after the beasts, represents 'the saints of the Most High' – the pious Jews who had become rebels under the Maccabees. When Jesus quotes this prophecy, he claims that his own cause is the cause of 'the saints of the Most High'; and he claims that the Most High, the Ancient of Days, will for this reason make clear the kingship over the nations to which he was called at his baptism.

Fortunately we need not discuss here whether the historical Jesus thought of himself as Messiah or Son of Man, or whether he wished to be called by these titles, and if so in what sense. Nor need we investigate the origins of such titles. *Messiah* meant 'the anointed' and 'Son of Man' meant 'the man' – and many ideas, Jewish or Gentile, about an anointed king, or about a man who was typical of others, might have fed the development of the Jewish hope that a great king would come on earth and a great man in the clouds. The scholars actively debate such subjects – and presumably will always do so, for the surviving evidence is ambiguous. What we can know is that Jesus implied a great claim by what he said and did, and that no one about whom we know anything was expecting a man who made that claim. Many theories about the coming Messiah or the heavenly Son of Man were in the Apocalyptic air at that time. None fitted the Jesus who came.

Nor need we discuss the many guesses which have been made about when and how Jesus would stage his 'Second Coming'. None of these guesses has turned out to be right so far. Were they misled by the very idea of 'coming'? Did Jesus promise a *parousia* or coming on earth, or did he imagine himself (or another Son of Man) as 'coming' from the earth to the Ancient of Days, or did the idea of a descent from heaven meet the idea of an ascent from the earth in the clouds? We do not know, for Jesus, being a poet, may have held together ideas which were contradictory in logic – and the only evidence about his imagination has come through the minds of the early Christians who (as we have seen) held a number of hopes.

What we can know is that these early Christians were driven by their own real experience to say that they believed that the future belonged to Jesus, that as history unfolded it would turn out to be the story of his coronation. All Christians who have in any way shared that experience have been driven to repeat the basic creed that 'Jesus is Lord'. Christians have said this because they have known the victory of Jesus, and because they have seen the future as well as the past in the light of that piece of knowledge in which reality itself seemed to lie disclosed. In the first letter attributed to St Peter, the future is described as the time 'when Jesus Christ is revealed' (I Pet. 1.7, 13), 'when his glory is revealed' (4.13). The early Christians may have imagined that glory in the shape of a Lamb on a throne, or in the shape of a Rider on a horse (Rev. 19.11-16), or in the shape of a Son of Man 'coming' to the earth, as he had first 'come' to the Ancient of Days, on the clouds (Acts 1.11). The images do not really matter. What matters is the all but totally incredible faith that the future will reveal, as the embodiment of humanity's dreams and God's purposes, one who suffered under Pontius Pilate, was crucified, dead and buried.

2 *Signs of the New Creation*

Nineteen hundred years have gone by, and Jesus Christ has not come – in the shape they expected. Has he come at all?

Many of those who have followed Jesus Christ into that future, as St Peter and St John were commanded to follow him according to the fourth gospel (John 21.18-23), have found that he has come to them in the way described in that gospel (John 14-17). He has come to give to the disciple a sense of trust because that disciple has already in some sense 'seen' the Father in Jesus; a new power and vitality in a new love; a peace 'such as the world cannot give', leading to a complete joy; a capacity both to bear 'fruit that shall last' and to endure the hatred of the world; a progress 'into all the truth'; a unity with other disciples as intimate as the unity of Jesus with his Father; a glory which is a foretaste of eternity. Here is the story of the Christian saints. It is the story of a force greater than the legions of Rome, the story of a golden thread through dark ages, the story of what was best in Christendom from St Francis to Martin Luther, the story of a fellowship which has come to include sober citizens of industrial states and spiritual nobles from all over Asia and Africa. It is a story to which the twentieth century has added chapters as great as any in the past.

But the sanctification of a tiny minority was not what Jesus lived and died for, and was not what the saints themselves most wanted. At the beginning the aim was clear, and that aim has been remembered in Christian history, often by mechanical repetition but sometimes in a leap of understanding and commitment:

> Father, thy name be hallowed;
> Thy kingdom come! (Luke 11.2)

And the tragedy of St John's writings (as of many later works of piety) was the narrowing of the horizon from the kingdom of God on earth to the sanctification of a minority.

With an insight born out of a deeply Christian courage, St John responded to the crisis caused by the deaths of those who had walked with Jesus and who had hoped for the kingdom to come visibly while they were still alive. He showed how the kingdom of God was among them, as in the days when Jesus performed earlier 'signs'. At the same time St John met creatively the challenge of translating the Gospel out of the thought-world of the Jew into the thought-world of the Greek. He made no substantial concessions to the powerful movement of Gnosticism, which pretended to possess a secret, mystical knowledge (*gnosis*) and which despised the facts of history and the flesh. Jesus Christ, he taught with a passionate emphasis, had come in the flesh – in Jewish flesh. But through his own spiritual and intellectual genius St John drew out of the Jewish thought-world, and out of the tradition about what the carpenter of Nazareth had said, precisely those elements which the Greek, and even the Gnostic, mind could understand – the teachings announced in the first five verses of his gospel, about the Reason in all things, about the Life which was the light of all men, about the Light which 'shone on' in the darkness of this world. So Greek pilgrims to Jerusalem, if they wished, could 'see Jesus' (John 12.21).

But St John's thought was not flawless. He wrote at a time when to the other problems of the Christian Church had been added the agony of its expulsion from the Jewish community. The Jews had been the people of God since the call to Abraham. Even the Roman state recognized the austere purity of their worship of God, at a time when Christians were believed to be incestuous cannibals (because of rumours about the Eucharist), enemies of society likely to commit arson or treason, and atheists who worshipped a criminal on a cross. But instead of welcoming, sheltering and hearing the greatest of its prophets and his disciples, the Jewish community had handed both Jesus and the Christians over to the ignorant and brutal 'justice' of Rome. The Jews' own defiance of Rome had come in the form of a senseless political rebellion, which had brought massacre and misery to the Holy Land and complete destruction to the Holy City and its temple.

In the Revelation of St John the Divine we see the over-flow of a Christian's bitterness against Rome, that new Babylon which was like a whore 'drunk with the blood of God's people' (Rev. 17.6). 'Pay her back in her own coin!' (Rev. 18.6). And in the gospel of St John the Evangelist we see the cold hatred of a Christian for the Jews. 'You will die in your sin; where I am going you cannot come. . . . Your father is the Devil and you choose to carry out your father's desires' (John 8.21, 44). Here the loyalty of Jesus of Nazareth to his own Jewish people, the neighbourliness which Jesus had extended to the Samaritans, and the love which he had extended to enemies, were narrowed down into a 'love of the brethren' – a love of other Christians. The disciples were to love one another, knowing that 'we are of God's family, while the whole godless world lies in the power of the evil one' (I John 5.19).

Many evils have therefore been encouraged by St John's

gospel. The tragic monstrosity of Christian anti-semitism (a foul blot on the Middle Ages and on our own time) can appeal to text after text in this gospel of love. Any Christian inclined to escape from the world, its problems and duties, into the cosy emotionalism of a pious clique feels entitled to drool over the farewell discourses at the last supper.

> We are the chosen few,
> All others will be damned;
> There is no room in heaven for you,
> We can't have heaven crammed.

And the Church, for all its grateful love for St John's gospel, has in its best moments known that here it was not the Gospel of Jesus. Indeed, the Church has preserved a better tradition in the other gospels, and with it some of the rebukes of Jesus to those who narrowed God's mercies. 'Then came the sons of Zebedee, James and his brother John, to whom he gave the name Boanerges, Sons of Thunder' (Mark 3.17). 'The disciples James and John . . . said, "Lord, may we call down fire from heaven to burn them up?" But he turned and rebuked them, and they went on to another village' (Luke 9.54–56).

In all the villages and cities of the world where the message of Jesus has been heard through the years called *Anno Domini*, a 'harvest of the Spirit' has grown. If this growth of virtues has been less remarkable than the sanctity of the outstanding saints, it has also included less fanaticism and less condemnation of the ordinary. If its love has been less intense, it has been broader. It has known happiness under great difficulties, if not a complete joy; and an inner peace, even if the world has not been completely renounced. Towards awkward Christians, and towards non-Christians, too, it has exercised 'patience, kindness, goodness, fidelity . . . and self-control' (Gal. 5.22). This growth of Christian character has, indeed, been wider than the active membership of the Christian Church. Hindus in India, and agnostic Humanists in the secular West, in many quiet ways have been influenced by the moral example of the Jesus whom they have usually acknowledged as at least 'a good man'. No other man in history has had this world-wide moral influence.

Can we, therefore, say that in changing the attitudes of these millions, Jesus has come back to this earth as clearly as he ever will? Is the kingdom best imagined in Sir Cecil Spring-Rice's hymn ('I vow to thee, my country . . .') about this spiritual community?

> We may not count her armies, we may not see her king,
> Her fortress is a faithful heart, her pride is suffering;
> And soul by soul and silently her shining bounds increase,
> And her ways are ways of gentleness and all her paths are peace.

We can put our question by citing one of the greatest theologians of the twentieth century (and one of the greatest of all commentators on St John's gospel) – Rudolf Bultmann. Bultmann developed a new interpretation of the word 'eschatological'. That word had been used in traditional theology to refer to 'the occurrences with which our known world comes to an end'.[4] Bultmann used it to refer to the moment of decision at the very beginning of Christian faith, the moment when a Christian puts his trust in God rather than in the things of this world. Bultmann also used it to refer to subsequent moments when, in a fresh crisis, the Christian has to choose in a fresh way between this world and the 'beyond'. And Bultmann used it also to refer to those moments in the Bible's story which present an attentive hearer with the choice of interpretation. *Either* this moment is a moment of triumph for the things of this world, for the world's strengths and delights and for its anxieties and sorrows, for its life and death; *or* this moment is a moment when the appeal of the eternal 'beyond' is seen as stronger than all the world. The chief of such 'eschatological' moments was for Bultmann the crucifixion of Jesus, which Christian faith sees as the tragic but pregnant end of all the old world; and this rising of faith in the crucified Jesus was Easter.

Bultmann put forward this Gospel as his interpretation of the pictures of the end in the New Testament, which he correctly described as 'mythological'. It was an interpretation which owed much to Bultmann's colleague in the University of Marburg, the philosopher Martin Heidegger. In the first chapter of this book we mentioned Heidegger's emphasis that 'authentic existence' can begin only when a man has come to terms with his approaching death. Bultmann saw this modern philosophy as a preparation for the Gospel, and taught that a man must choose between the attractiveness of this world, which turns out to be its anxiety because everything in it dies, and 'authentic existence' based on faith in the eternal 'beyond'. As he said: 'You must look into your own personal history. Always in your present moment lies the meaning of history, and you cannot see it as a spectator, but only in your responsible decisions. In every moment slumbers the possibility of being the eschatological moment. You must awaken it.'[5] Such a message was especially relevant to many Germans and to many others also, at a time when the proud world of Europe lay in the ruins of war and when anxiety was often followed by despair.

But many Christians have also seen that even the spiritual harvest of love, joy, peace and the other lovely virtues, or even an 'existential' trust in the 'beyond' amid anxiety and despair, could never be enough to fulfil the Church's original hope. These quiet, spiritual realities *are* more important than dramatic miracles or fabulous myths – but they are not the 'last things' about which the New Testament spoke. They are human reactions to the evil in the world. 'Her pride is suffering', his decision is for faith rather than despair – but the world remains evil, the source of suffering and anxiety. This message, although it is a noble message, is not a full interpretation of the New Testament's often repeated proclamation that the evil in *the world is being conquered*, that what is really wrong is being changed, that voices can already be heard in heaven shouting: 'The sovereignty of the world has passed to our Lord and his Christ, and he shall reign for ever and ever!' (Rev. 11.15). And many have wondered whether the voice of Rudolf

Bultmann echoes that triumphant shout when he modestly says: 'Christian hope knows *that* it hopes, but it does not know what it hopes for.'[6]

The New Testament, in fact, teaches clearly *a hope for history*, not an escape from it into a private religion. The New Testament, on the whole, neither accepts nor rejects the world. It announces that it is being changed. For this reason St Augustine, in the years of our Lord 413–427, wrote down his vision of the Catholic Church as the embodiment of the kingdom of God on earth. Just as he had come to think that his own flesh, which had led him into so many sins and which he had so often rejected in self-disgust, would be redeemed and raised at the end, so he came to see that the empire of Rome, which had inflicted such persecutions on the Church and which had now itself fallen to the barbarians, was not the last great political system to rule the world. While the city of Rome was in flames, the enduring and expanding Church effectively (although not perfectly) represented the City of God on earth. It must do so, for a gospel had promised that the Church would be unique among the world's institutions. 'The forces of death shall never overpower it' (Matt. 16.18).[7]

St Augustine's *City of God* encouraged the Christendom of the Middle Ages. But the Catholic Church grew corrupt, and that Christendom died. At the Reformation of the sixteenth century, men therefore turned back to the older vision of the Church as no more than one human sign of God's kingship. Since then Protestants – and gradually many Roman Catholics also – have subordinated the Church to the kingdom, believing that the cause of the Church is great, but that the Church's purpose is to announce and to serve a greater cause: the cause of God's kingdom in the world.

This is the vision of the Church which the New Testament gives in the letter to Ephesus (where, according to tradition, St John's gospel was written) Here life in the Church is seen as the revelation to believers of God's 'hidden purpose . . . namely, that the universe, all in heaven and on earth, might be brought into a unity in Christ' (Eph. 1.10). In a daring speculation, the writer adds that even 'the rulers and authorities in the realms of heaven' are to learn about this future from the Church (Eph. 3.10). No greater role is possible for the Church than to be by its true glory – not by its visible power, or by its appeal to public opinion – the sign of the coming renewal and reunion of the whole of God's creation. To be a real member of the Church, a Christian must be a personal example of the newness which is to renew everything later. 'The only thing that counts is new creation' (Gal. 6.15), for 'when anyone is united to Christ, there is a new world' (II Cor. 5.17). The Christian must be a walking sign of this new world. The Church is the place where all may learn God's promise and look forward to 'new heavens and a new earth, the home of justice' (II Pet. 3.13).

3 *God's Way of Progress*

How is God fulfilling his promise to his whole creation, the promise which Christians have heard through their own experience of personal renewal?

Wisely, the New Testament does not include a history of the universe written beforehand. But it does include some visions which interpret a current crisis as a disclosure of God's way of working. The Revelation of St John the Divine, probably springing out of the Roman rulers' demand that the Christians of Asia Minor should reverence the emperor Domitian as 'Lord and God', is a vision of the whole conflict between the one true God and his enemies. This conflict is so great that it cannot be quick, but the end is sure. This kind of vision is 'Apocalyptic', in that (like the Book of Daniel) it comments on the present by means of an elaborate vision of the future. Such Apocalyptic literature also emphasizes that the evil on earth is so great that a divine intervention will be necessary to bring in a new order.

Inevitably, much in this literature strikes us as bizarre nonsense. It was (it would appear) easy when writing in the

Apocalyptic style to slip into the habit of producing page after page of detail about the divine intervention which was to come and about the new age which was to follow. Perhaps this sort of thing, like the background detail in a modern novel, was never intended to do more than to entertain. Archdeacon R. H. Charles, who was more learned in this ancient literature than anyone before or after him in Britain, was a modernist in his personal faith and revealed that he despised much of the material to which he gave a lifetime of study. He dismissed much of it as 'puerilities and absurdities', and would lament that 'eschatological beliefs are universally the last of all beliefs to be influenced by the loftier conceptions of God'.[8] Bishop Gore, who thought R. H. Charles 'over-enthusiastic' about this specialism, quoted an American writer with approval: 'The world was to come to an end. But what really did come to an end in that literature was the last shred of thinking capacity and common sense.'[9] Today scholars are humbler – and this is not only because few of them have spent as much time on this literature as R. H. Charles did. They are not so sure that it was fundamentally absurd. It kept the courage of Jews and Christians high under almost intolerable pressures. In our time of dramas to which 'common sense' may be an inadequate response, this literature of despair and faith may have something to say to us.

If we really do feel ourselves superior to the Apocalyptic elements in the New Testament, we may still find much material for our sympathetic study in its *prophetic* elements – in those less elaborately futuristic and less copiously miraculous visions or flashes of insight, where the New Testament is in the great tradition of the prophets of the Old (echoing, for example, the prophet in Babylon, Isa. 40–55, whose exultant songs about deliverance and home-coming supplied much of the imagery of the Christian hope).

One emphasis in the New Testament is on *the self-effacement and the patience of God*. This emphasis is strong in St John the Divine's account of the wrongdoing in the

Roman empire, but it also comes in the parables of Jesus, as when Jesus compares God with a man who leaves his home for a long journey (Mark 13.34, etc.) or with one of the many absentee owners of Palestinian vineyards (Mark 12.1, etc.). This emphasis is, of course, highly relevant to the twentieth century. We open our newspapers and find that evil is violent and unchecked. We open our science books and read about the immense ages in the story of evolution, and about the apparent dominance of chance and waste. We have every reason to agree with the New Testament that, if God is real, he is at present so hidden that it often seems as if he were absent on a long journey. How remote both from our own world-view and from the world-view of the New Testament are the complacent philosophies of some other periods! Even thoughtful people in those periods calmly assumed that nature was already neatly ordered in order to meet all man's needs. We and the New Testament, on the other hand, view reality as at present largely a chaos.

The New Testament knows almost no limits to the power of man to bring good out of this chaos. The parables just mentioned picture the world as like a great house being run by the servants, or like a farm where the tenants are extremely confident. While God is obscure and seems absent, men are to put their talents, the capital entrusted to them, to a highly profitable use (Matt. 25.14–30). The idea goes back to the Old Testament's picture of Adam as God's deputy on earth, the viceroy over the rest of creation (Gen. 1.28). The New Testament is itself a story of the great things which men can do, a success story. The twentieth century, which is an age of intoxicating achievements and revolutionary expectations, knows something of this thrill of a new start for man and something of this hope of an even greater glory to come. We know that, despite all the delays and reverses, progress has been real so far, and will accelerate fantastically unless we ruin it. We also know that modern progress made its breakthrough in a Europe and North America which had been saturated by Christian teaching. Was there any connection between that teaching and the energetic optimism of European and North American civilization? Some historians have traced connections between the rise of modern science and the biblical belief in a world which was important (because God had made it 'good', and because men were appointed stewards over it) but not sacred (because God was not in it as a pagan god might be in a rock or stream or sky or wind). Some historians have also said that the restless, pushful Europeans and North Americans who considered themselves the lords of creation owed something to their Christian background, while also disgracing it; and that Karl Marx and Sigmund Freud did belong to Israel. Fortunately we do not have to explore the many problems involved. The point for us is that we can hear a blessing on human progress in the Bible, and we can know that Revolution is the twentieth-century word which best translates the biblical hope for man on earth.

But another great biblical emphasis is on *the apparent triumph of evil*. This comes out in the question of how best to interpret a famous verse in the letter to the Romans (8.28). Did St Paul promise here that 'all things work together for good for those who love God'? Or, as the New English Bible prefers, did he merely say out of his own experience that in everything the Spirit 'co-operates for good with those who love God'? The gospels contain three fairly long Apocalyptic visions. All are attributed to Jesus and they probably reflect some of his own warnings about the things which would work *against* his disciples. In their present forms they spring chiefly out of the Christians' profound alarm at the Jewish rebellion and the destruction of Jerusalem. 'Those days will bring distress such as never has been until now' is the warning in St Mark's gospel (13.19), and later evangelists, writing after the disaster, had to adjust St Mark's material only in details (Matt. 24; Luke 21). Such visions are the reverse of a liberal optimism about an inevitable progress. They foretell, or react to, a catastrophe.

The New Testament thus warns us that some things will get worse before they get better – and it adds that some of the catastrophes will be caused by good things going very wrong. The apparent triumph of evil is to be the Christian's way of knowing that the 'Day of the Lord' is at hand. This warning was made vivid by the mythological figure of Antichrist, the great enemy who was to appear before Christ reappeared. 'The Day of the Lord,' St Paul warned, 'cannot come before the final rebellion against God, when wickedness will be revealed in human form, the man doomed to perdition. He is the Enemy. He rises in his pride against every god, so called, every object of men's worship, and even takes his seat in the temple of God, claiming to be a god himself' (II Thess. 2.2–4). Many Christians have tried to spot this Antichrist. St John the Divine thought he had spotted him in the Roman emperor, and so apparently did St John the Evangelist, who wrote to his disciples, 'You were told that Antichrist was to come, and now many antichrists have appeared; which proves to us that this is indeed the last hour' (I John 2.18). Martin Luther believed that the Pope was Antichrist, and drew a similar conclusion about the end being near – a belief and a conclusion shared by many later Protestants.

Few Christians nowadays take the prophecy of Antichrist literally, but everyone in the twentieth century has the best reason to know that progress carries with it the possibility of catastrophe. Progress is real – but does not bring an automatic salvation.

This is, indeed, the theme of our century. A technically advanced civilization may use all its skills to commit suicide in total war. Medical victories over death may cause massive famines. Urbanization may corrupt and choke our cities. Industrial technology may poison or exhaust the earth's resources. The struggle to build strong nations with social justice may bring tyrannies worse than any emperor's or any pope's. A revolution may eat its own children. Mass communication may trivialize life and make a people uniform for political or commercial purposes. Cybernetics may dehumanize more poisonously than the first industrial revolution. And these are not remote possibilities. The nuclear bombers already fly overhead; the missiles have their targets; the mouths likely to starve are born; our cities can already be hells; some natural resources are already under threat; the cruelties of Nazism and Communism are familiar; *1984* as the aftermath of revolution often seems near. . . . Secular people themselves tend to be anti-utopian nowadays. And nothing in Christianity entitles us to believe that a particular catastrophe will be averted miraculously. The God who did not send legions of angels to Calvary is not likely to catch a hydrogen bomb before it falls on New York. Christianity, a religion signed with the sign of the cross, is full of tragedies. Not one stone of Jerusalem was left on another. The famous churches of Asia Minor and North Africa, where St John the Divine and St Augustine saw their visions of the City of God, were practically obliterated by Islam. . . . By now, Christians should have learned not to commit their hearts to any institution, not even to a church – for any institution in history can perish either because of attack by a greater power or because of its own inner corruption. Their vision of life should be 'eschatological' and therefore somewhat detached. 'Mourners should be as if they had nothing to grieve them, the joyful as if they did not rejoice' (I Cor. 7.30). When terrors and disasters are near, Christians should remember that what the New Testament does say as the fall of Jerusalem approaches is this: 'You be on your guard; I have forewarned you of it all' (Mark 13.23).

The New Testament thus provides no authority for the speculation that the Christian Church – or what is sometimes more vaguely referred to as 'Christian civilization' – will inevitably expand to cover the earth and include the whole of mankind. This hope has been held by many Europeans and North Americans in the nineteenth and twentieth centuries. Before Auschwitz and Hiroshima, the civilization of the white races seemed so obviously superior to all others that its religion was bound to prevail, particularly since the religion (or rather, a copiously watered down version of it) was so obviously true. All that was needed was a bit of a push.

> March we forth in the strength of God with the banner of Christ unfurled. . . .
> Fight we the fight with sorrow and sin, to set their captives free. . . .
> Yet nearer and nearer draws the time, the time that shall surely be,
> When the earth shall be filled with the knowledge of God as the waters cover the sea.

But somehow the march to Utopia got halted because 'sorrow and sin' were seen to reign in the Christian army, and in a more sober frame of mind Christians opened their Bibles again, finding there a hope which was far from utopian.

We have already said that the New Testament is a success story, for it records the acts of the apostles, the spread of the Gospel from Jerusalem to Rome, the growth of the mustard-tree 'for the birds to come and roost among its branches' (Matt. 13.32). But St Paul, writing to Rome, outlined a missionary strategy where there was not a trace of belief in a gradual, inevitable triumph. It was a strategy of mission to the Gentiles, gathering those in each city whom God would make Christians, in the hope that these signs of the reconciliation of the whole world to God would stir up the Jews so that God could once again 'accept' his ancient people. But St Paul did not believe that the goal of this mission, the conversion of Israel, would be reached before the resurrection at the end of history. 'For if their rejection has meant the reconciliation of the world, what will their acceptance mean? Nothing less than life from the dead!' (Rom. 11.15) St Mark also believed that 'before the end the Gospel must be proclaimed to all nations' (Mark 13.10), but not that the Church would be victorious in all nations; the angels, not the missionaries, would gather God's chosen 'from the farthest bounds of earth' (Mark 13.27). St Luke, the poetic theologian of the mission to all men, could find it a real question: 'When the

Son of Man comes, will he find faith on earth?' (Luke 18.8). So when persecution rather than triumph met the preaching of the Gospel, the Christians of the New Testament knew that they had been forewarned.

In the period into which we are now moving, Christianity may be the most vigorous and successful of the world's religions. It is already the largest. Despite its handicaps in the middle of the twentieth century (for example, its identification with colonialism), Christianity seems able to live with technical, intellectual and social progress (for example, in the United States), and religions which have been less involved in the creation of the modern world (for example, Buddhism) seem less competent. But the handicaps may prove greater than the advantages for Christianity in Asia and Africa; and in Europe and America (North and South) secularism may prevail as the heir of Christianity. There are already many ominous signs of Christianity's defeat; perhaps in the period into which we are now moving the Church may everywhere be reduced to a small minority. If Christians do experience this as their immediate future, the New Testament will have forewarned them.

When the final siege of Jerusalem was about to begin in AD 68, the Christians in the city fled to the town of Pella. They had been forewarned. The survival of that small religious community had no great significance in the march of history, for their half-Jewish version of Christianity dwindled and almost disappeared. They became the heretical Ebionites. But the escape of those few Christians from the fall of Jerusalem, and the strong survival in cities all around the Mediterranean of the Gospel which had first been preached in Jerusalem, have come to represent the whole fulfilment of God's promises to those who heed his warnings. The little Apocalypse in St Mark's gospel, after all its warnings, had promised: 'After that distress . . . then they will see the Son of Man coming in the clouds with great power and glory' (Mark 13.24, 26). When Jerusalem had fallen to the Romans, history had not turned out quite like that. But a Christian writing 'to the Hebrews' – to fellow-Christians tempted to revert to being Jews in order to escape Roman persecution – could now claim that 'the kingdom we are given is unshakable' (Heb. 12.28), and could say that this kingdom still had a future. 'Let us be firm and unswerving in the confession of our hope, for the Giver of the promise may be trusted' (Heb. 10.23).

The God of the New Testament is a God who keeps his promise, if necessary after the worst catastrophe which the sin of man can cause. He is the God who raised Jesus from the dead. He is the God who delivered the Church from many dangers. If civilization commits global suicide, this God can be trusted to build a new civilization out of the human remnants on the earth. If no faith is left on earth, this God can still be trusted to make all of humanity that lives into his eternal Church. If no men are left – for the earth will eventually become uninhabitable, and at present it seems that it will not be possible to begin the human story again on another planet – this God can still be trusted to 'raise' his creation eternally. The old Jerusalem will fall, but the new Jerusalem will contain all that was good in it – and more. This new Jerusalem will not be built by man, for the kingdom of God will not be brought about by human effort. The eternal City which is to include all of a redeemed history will come from God (Rev. 21.2).

Like the God of the burning bush, the God of the New Testament is thus a God of promise, a God of the future. He will show who he is by what he will do. But the New Testament is far more boldly confident than the Old. It may, indeed, be regarded as the outline of a solution to the Old Testament's unanswered problem about how God's promises are to come true. The New Testament knows that Easter after Good Friday 'is the Yes pronounced upon God's promises, every one of them' (II Cor. 1.20). For Christians now, history is essentially the time between the first Easter and the end. It is 'the time between the times', to use a phrase which Karl Barth made famous. The whole universe is the scene and the instrument of the completion of God's triumph in Christ: the universe is in the old phrase the 'theatre of glory' – but is also the glorious drama itself. It is therefore possible to think of Christ as the clue to the whole story, to think of the future as being Christ-shaped, and to think of history and of nature as material nearly red-hot with Christ, waiting to flame up (to use a comparison often elaborated by Pierre Teilhard de Chardin).

Dr Hendrikus Berkhof has put clearly what a modern man may make of this New Testament hope:

> Jesus Christ is final because he is on the way to his final victory. He is God's guarantee and down-payment, and therefore our great sign of hope. Christians do not differ from others as if they had reached the goal. Together with all men we remain on the journey, *in via.* But we know that there is a goal and a way. Though we cannot offer final solutions for the endless problems of our un-redeemed world, nevertheless in the resurrection of Jesus we have discovered the direction in which God leads, and the ground and inspiration for an unceasing struggle for renewal. That is more modest than what we have often pretended to possess, but it is real and sufficient.[10]

When the men who wrote the New Testament amid great problems and sufferings were asked *how* the final triumph after the chaos and the catastrophe was guaranteed, they simply said: in Jesus Christ and the Spirit he gives. And when they were asked *why* the triumph was sure, they simply said: because it so pleases the Father. We may be able to enter into this strange world of thought if we compare the infinite pleasure of God with our pleasure in good memories. We are enriched by our memories. In some way beyond our imagining, God is enriched by the completion of his purposes in the life of Jesus and, eventually, in the life of the universe. Even the eternal God, who is already rich in a joy beyond all our imaginings, will be fuller when he, who 'is love', has created and brought his creation to its triumphant conclusion in eternal glory, in the 'universal restoration' (Acts 3.21). It is because this pleases the Ancient of Days that the Son of Man will rise above tragedy and bring all saints, all men, all things with him.

Thus the New Testament told men that 'their Maker will not fail them' (I Pet. 4.19). The power of this faithful Creator to bring good out of evil, and the trust which the believer ought to have in this ability of God to make the best of things – these were the themes of the New Testament. They embraced the whole of history in the whole of nature. They held good for the existence which men knew in time and space, and for eternity. But the vision of the New Testament was never airborne. It ended by asking the believer to trust God in his own life. The promise that 'their Maker will not fail them' was made to Christians who were about to suffer because they were Christians, in a 'fiery ordeal' (I Pet. 4.12–16).

In our time, Christians are again being called upon to suffer material loss, social disgrace, physical punishment and death, like their predecessors in first-century Rome. The twentieth century has already produced far more recruits for the noble army of the Church's martyrs than any previous century. But in our time there is also another form of suffering which tests Christians. Ours is a time when the belief in the divine, the hope that human life will be fulfilled in heaven, the trust in a glorious conclusion to the whole cosmic enterprise – a belief taken for granted by most men in history – has been eclipsed for many by the pressures and the questions of the present world. Many who would wish to be reckoned as Christians have to find their ways into the Christian tradition by slow steps, each one of which demands a courageous defiance of current intellectual fashions. It may be necessary for them to remain for many years, or for a whole lifetime, in a position of being fascinated by Jesus while unable to accept fully his teaching about God and eternity. Many such people would, however, say that they would choose the side of Jesus rather than the side of his enemies, even if his crucifixion was the end. Such modern disciples may have to enter the experience of the men of the Old Testament, who for centuries were fascinated by Yahweh, and who worshipped him, without being able to believe that he could offer them a heavenly reward. That may be the school through which faith has to go in our time. But whether they suffer physically or intellectually, Christians can at least know what it would be like, to be confident about Jesus Christ and his future and his Father. And, resolved to be 'with Jesus' whether for eternal life or for eternal death, they can ask to be given that confidence by the Father. Perhaps they will repeat for themselves the prayer of St Paul towards the end of his life: 'All I care for is to know Christ, to experience the power of his resurrection, and to share his sufferings, in growing conformity with his death, if only I may finally arrive at the resurrection from the dead . . . I press on, hoping to take hold of that for which Christ once took hold of me' (Phil. 3.11, 12).

It seems necessary for the Christian Church to find room in its ranks for many people who want to be there in order to fight in the struggles of life, but who are unable to give their full assent to the Church's traditional creed about eternity, or to its basis in the New Testament. Presumably there have always been half-believers who lived and died as Christians in each generation since Christianity entered the world, and the Church has been merciful enough not to inquire too closely into the extent to which they were orthodox while living or dying. In their thousands or millions, they have been covered by the compassion of Jesus for the man who cried to him: 'I have faith; help me where faith falls short' (Mark 9.24). But in our time the eternal background of life – that mysterious dimension where everything is possible (Mark 9.23) is concealed for many by the bright lights shining, or by the sordid little dramas being enacted on the stage; and in such a time as this, an acknowledgment of the psychological situation of half-belief is needed urgently. The Church must be tender towards modern men who listen to the tragedy of Jesus without being able to hear the laughter of God at Easter – who hold out their hands to receive the bread which symbolizes the life and death of the best of mankind's prophets, without being ready for a communion with the Christ who is said by the Church's poetry to be enthroned 'far beyond the skies'. The Church must be willing to bury the body and to comfort the mourners when the dying person has expressed a religious attitude falling far short of the faith demanded in the old Prayer Books, and when the mourners stand around the grave or at the crematorium with little more than an awed perplexity in their hearts. The sheer willingness to be counted a Christian must very often be allowed to outweigh a tongue-tied bewilderment.

However, to plead for patience and tolerance towards the unorthodox who wish to identify themselves with the Christian Church, or to argue (as has been argued in this book) that the Church needs to restate its own orthodoxy by abandoning dead phrases such as the 'resurrection of the body', does not necessarily involve the suggestion that the transcendent mystery towards which those old orthodox words tried to point should be abandoned. For the Christian Gospel shows us this mystery; it simply cannot be stated in an exclusively secular way.

On the contrary, it is now more than ever important that the depths of the mystery surrounding human life should be acknowledged as an integral part of true humanism, and it is more than ever important that a full statement of Christianity should be seen to include the claim that the light and life coming to us through Jesus Christ come in grace from this mystery. What has happened in the twentieth century has been the widespread, almost universal, adoption of parts of the Christian doctrine of 'the last things', omitting the eternal God who is declared by Christianity to be the Alpha and the Omega, the A and the Z, of all things. The modern situation arises from a wish to have the Christian energy without the Christian motivation, the Christian hope without the Christian faith, which is like wanting butter without bread or flowers without roots. And what has happened to the modern world is remarkably like what happens to a child who eats butter without its tedious foundation, or what happens to flowers when they are cut to display their beauty indoors.

The whole modern movement which for the first time is pulling all the peoples of the world into a single history was originally inspired by the belief that man was already glorious and was on his way to further glories. This belief was inspired in its turn by a belief in God as the Father of man – a belief which owes much to Greece, and more to Israel, but more still to the Christian Church as the mother of Europe. Largely because the custodians of this religious vision of man betrayed one or other aspect of their heritage, it was necessary for many of the makers of the modern world to be (at least in their own eyes) anti-religious or at least anti-clerical. Thus Gibbon stressed rationality as the greatest ornament of a civilization, and saw the 'barefooted fryars' as trampling on the ruins of reason. Freud stressed the freedom of love as the fulfilment of life, and saw the morality of civilization, with its religious supports, as repressing it. Marx saw the progress of the people as the plot of the entire historical drama, and saw religious preachers among the villains. Lord Acton, a devout Roman Catholic, felt compelled to oppose his own ecclesiastical hierarchy in the nineteenth century for the sake of truth and liberty. Yet in the original vision, reason and love were held together as aspects of the 'image of God' in man, and progress towards liberty was promised to all the sons of God who were being brought by the divine plan towards their liberation and glory. Because the religious vision of man has been discredited and broken in this way, the modern world has been compelled to worship reason or love, progress or liberty as a kind of secular god.

It would indeed be foolish for religious believers to attempt to condemn, or to denigrate, the chapter about atheism in the history of the world; but it is fair to recall that it is a short chapter and an anxious one. Those who believe that the old description of man as the child of God was basically true cannot be surprised to see the spiritual disasters which have followed the modern vision of man without God, and even those who believe that eternity is a fiction admit many of the problems. Reason has very often degenerated into a sterile intellectualism, and love into a subhuman lust. The progress of the people has crushed the happiness of the individual, or the individual's liberty has produced anarchy. And where there has been no belief in the eternal God as a source of wisdom and strength, there has been – for so many, in the end – little hope that these fundamental problems which man has brought upon himself can be solved in time to avert catastrophe. We are, of course, not claiming that all atheists are miserable, or that religious belief has been exempt from great corruptions. All that we are doing is to point to certain well-known problems in the spiritual life of modern man, and to include among those problems the decline in the contemporary West of the hitherto almost universal belief that eternity surrounds man. We can try to be fair to the achievements of our time, and to be candid about religion's immense failures, while maintaining that the quality, and even the survival, of human life on this planet should be a subject for concern and should be regarded as bound up with the recovery of the religious vision.

What is at at stake now includes a crisis of belief in man, as well as a crisis of belief in God. There are already many signs of a tendency in the most sensitive observers of our time to depict man as an ultimately helpless animal. This animal, this 'naked ape', may well pick up a lot of pleasure on the way to his doom, but that does not release him from the trap. This animal may well be unique among animals because he understands his tragedy, but that does not prevent the tragedy happening. Such a tendency to view man as the tragic animal needs to be answered by those who have glimpsed the heights to which the human powers of reason and love may progress in liberty; and it may well be that, in the final analysis, it can be answered only by those who can see the everlasting arms of God sustaining man. At the end of his *Life of Gladstone*, first published in 1903, the agnostic Lord Morley paid a superb tribute to the dead statesman's human qualities 'of public duty and of private faithfulness'. Morley made no secret either of the fact that the whole of Gladstone's life was controlled by his religious belief, or of his own scepticism about that belief. He hoped that lives of Gladstone's quality would be lived after the collapse of Gladstone's creed. In conclusion he quoted Gladstone: 'Be inspired with the belief that life is a great and noble calling; not a mean and grovelling thing, that we are to shuffle through as we can, but an elevated and lofty destiny.' The great question of our time is: was Gladstone or Morley right about the source of man's calling and destiny?

Those who reject the religious vision of human glory argue that it is too good to be true – that the real truth is unpleasant: namely, death. And this suspicion of the possibility that religion may be all a romantic illusion will probably always seem a natural suspicion, except in those rare moments of an individual's life when he is caught up into an ecstatic bliss and except in those rare moments of a people's story when the whole society is filled with a sense of harmony and well-being. Certainly in our own age, which is an age of acute anxiety, a cosmic optimism may seem implausible. But in our times of despair about the future we need to reflect how improbable was the course of evolution and of history in the past, as out of chaos progress came. When this planet formed out of cosmic dust (or however it did form), could a Martian observer have predicted the subsequent story? We should ourselves refuse to believe such a tale, were it not for the evidence. What religion does is to provide fresh evidence about the evolution and history of a man as a creature of God, made to worship God and to enjoy him for ever. For Christians, the most important evidence is, of course, the cluster of events around Christ. Those who do not soak themselves in this evidence, those who refuse to take religion seriously, naturally see nothing in it. But those of us who let this evidence tell its own story can let it contradict the scepticism which we imbibe from the society around us.

There is no way of forcing anyone to take the religious evidence seriously. Conversion to the religious view of human destiny comes about through an infection. One human being takes an interest in another; one human being is willing to consider the other's attitude; one human being is gradually persuaded by the other. Perhaps all that can be said to a person outside the brotherhood of religious belief is to ask that person why, in his total view of human destiny, he gives the moments of darkness which all men experience more importance than the moments of light. Amid the inexplicable tragedies of life, everyone is acquainted with joy, and often the joys are great. That is why, if given the choice, almost everyone prefers to go on living; and that is why many have believed that the moments of light and joy before death point to a glory beyond it, because those moments are the beginning of the conversation which the eternal God holds with man the 'naked ape'. But this appeal to a secular person's own experience is never a proof, and cannot be a merely intellectual argument. It *may* persuade at a level deeper than the level of argument, if the belief in a destiny of glory is embodied in a peace in one's own life. When heart speaks to heart, having this peace in oneself is the best way to follow the advice of the New Testament: 'Be always ready with your defence whenever you are called to account for the hope that is in you, but make that defence with modesty and respect' (I Pet. 3.15).

For us as for our predecessors, the test of whether we understand and believe the New Testament's doctrine about the 'last things' in time and eternity is how we live now, and how we prepare to die. Is it true about us, as it was about many of those first Christians, that we have let ourselves be gripped and held by Christ, and led by him into the undisclosed future of God? 'If we live, we live for the Lord; and if we die, we die for the Lord' (Rom. 14.8). 'There is nothing in death or life . . . , nothing in all creation that can separate us from the love of God in Christ Jesus our Lord' (Rom. 8.38, 39). 'Dying, we still live on; disciplined by suffering, we are not done to death; in our sorrows we have always cause for joy; poor ourselves, we bring wealth to many; penniless, we own the world' (II Cor. 6.10).

NOTES

1. For 'the psychoanalytical meaning of history', see Norman Brown, *Life against Death*, London: Routledge and Conn.: Wesleyan University Press, 1959.

2. G. P. Gooch, *History and Historians in the Nineteenth Century*, London: Longmans, 1913, p. 385.

3. See Mircea Eliade, *The Myth of the Eternal Return*, London: Routledge and New York: Panther Books, 1955.

4. Rudolf Bultmann, *History and Eschatology*, Edinburgh University Press, 1957, p. 23.

5. *History and Eschatology*, p. 155.

6. Walther Schmithals, *An Introduction to the Theology of Rudolf Bultmann*, London: SCM Press and Minneapolis: Augsburg Publishing Company, 1968, p. 323.

7. The theology of St Augustine has had to be mentioned superficially more than once, even in this short book. For the biography behind its subtleties see Peter Brown, *Augustine of Hippo*, London: Faber and Berkeley: University of California Press, 1967.

8. R. H. Charles, *The Resurrection of Man*, Edinburgh: T. and T. Clark, 1929, pp. 9, 35. An identical lament had appeared in his *Critical History of the Doctrine of a Future Life*, London: A. and C. Black, 1899, p. 310.

9. Charles Gore, *The Reconstruction of Belief*, London: John Murray, 1926, p. 317.

10. From an address at the Fourth Assembly of the World Council of Churches, Uppsala 1968. See his Bible studies prepared for an earlier ecumenical conference, in *Key Words of the Gospel*, London: SCM Press and Richmond, Virginia: John Knox Press, 1964.

For Further Reading

1 *Thoughts before Dying*

1. For a medical assessment with a good bibliography, see John Hinton, *Dying* (Pelican paperback, 1967), and for a sociological assessment, Geoffrey Gorer, *Death, Grief and Mourning* (Cresset Press, 1965). A good collection of essays is *Man's Concern with Death* by A. J. Toynbee and others (Hodder and Stoughton and McGraw–Hill Book Co., New York, 1968). The two books by Norman Auton, *The Pastoral Care of the Dying* and *The Pastoral Care of the Bereaved* (SPCK, 1966 and 1967), are based on experience as a hospital chaplain. A discussion of the twentieth-century climate of opinion is offered in David L. Edwards, *Religion and Change* (Hodder and Stoughton and Harper & Row, New York, 1969).

2. A convenient assembly of the texts is in C. Ryder Smith, *The Bible Doctrine of the Hereafter* (Epworth Press, 1958).

3. For a balanced introduction with a good bibliography, see D. J. West, *Psychical Research Today* (Pelican paperback, 1962). See also the two essays by Rosalind Heywood in *Man's Concern with Death*, cited above.

4. The commentaries show how many of the Old Testament texts can be interpreted in various senses, but see, e.g., R. Martin-Achard, *From Death to Life* (Oliver and Boyd, Edinburgh, 1960).

5–6. For an attack on the mind-body dualism, see Gilbert Ryle, *The Concept of Mind* (Hutchinson, 1949, and Barnes & Noble, New York, 1950); and for a Christian philosopher's treatment of some 'disclosure situations',

Ian T. Ramsey, *Freedom and Immortality* (SCM Press, 1960). For the other religions, see, e.g., *The Concise Encyclopaedia of Living Faiths*, ed. R. C. Zaehner (Hutchinson and Hawthorn Books, New York, 1959).

2 *The New Testament*

Popular fears and hopes in the past are illustrated in D. P. Walker, *The Decline of Hell* (Routledge and University of Chicago Press, 1964), and Norman Cohn, *The Pursuit of the Millennium* (Secker and Warburg and Essential Books, Inc., New York, 1957). But see also Ulrich Simon, *Heaven in the Christian Tradition* (Rockliff and Harper & Row, New York, 1958).

Recent scholarly discussion is surveyed in two books by Norman Perrin, *The Kingdom of God in the Teaching of Jesus* (SCM Press and Westminster Press, Philadelphia, 1963) and *Rediscovering the Teaching of Jesus* (SCM Press and Harper & Row, New York, 1967). Detailed treatments of the eschatology of Jesus include W. G. Kümmel, *Promise and Fulfilment* (SCM Press, 1957). Recent discussion also includes Michael Perry, *The Easter Enigma* (Faber, 1959); G. W. H. Lampe and D. M. MacKinnon, *The Resurrection* (Mowbray and Westminster Press, Philadelphia, 1967); and *The Significance of the Message of the Resurrection for Faith in Jesus Christ*, ed. C. F. D. Moule (SCM Press, 1968). For the Apocalyptic background, see D. S. Russell, *The Method and Message of Jewish Apocalyptic* (SCM Press and Westminster Press, Philadelphia, 1964); and for the motives of the Apostolic Age, see Ferdinand Hahn, *Mission in the New Testament* (SCM Press, 1965).

3 *Eternity in Christian Faith Today*

Non-technical treatments by Reformed theologians include John Baillie, *And the Life Everlasting* (Oxford University Press, 1934, and Scribners, New York, 1933), and Emil Brunner, *Eternal Hope* (Lutterworth Press and Westminster Press, Philadelphia, 1954). Recent Anglican discussion includes Ulrich Simon, *The End is Not Yet* (Nisbet, 1964);

Michael Paternoster, *Thou Art There Also* (SPCK, 1967); and John A. T. Robinson, *In the End, God* (Fontana paperback and Harper & Row, New York, 1968). An example of Conservative Evangelical teaching is J. A. Motyer, *After Death* (Hodder paperback and Westminster Press, Philadelphia, 1965).

4 *The Rising Man*

For the background, see Karl Löwith, *Meaning in History* (Chicago University Press, 1949), and Alan Richardson, *History, Sacred and Profane* (SCM Press and Westminster Press, Philadelphia, 1964). Three suggestive books about the gospels are D. E. Nineham, *St Mark* (Pelican paperback, 1963); Hans Conzelmann, *The Theology of St Luke* (Faber, 1960); and John Marsh, *St John* (Pelican paperback, 1968).

Recent theological discussion includes Hendrikus Berkhof, *Christ the Meaning of History* (SCM Press and John Knox Press, Richmond, Virginia, 1966); Jürgen Moltmann, *Theology of Hope* (SCM Press and Harper & Row, New York, 1967); Oscar Cullmann, *Salvation in History* (SCM Press and Harper & Row, New York, 1967); Ronald Gregor Smith, *The Free Man* (Collins and Westminster Press, Philadelphia, 1969). The conviction that historical progress does not guarantee redemption was stated eloquently by Reinhold Niebuhr in, e.g., his *Faith and History* (Nisbet and Scribners, New York, 1949). Since then there has been a return to Christian optimism, illustrated by the discussion around the Assembly of the World Council of Churches at Evanston in 1954 (specially by the report of its Preparatory Commission on *Christ the Hope of the World*; and by the influence of the Jesuit scientist, Pierre Teilhard de Chardin (see the biography by Robert Speaight, Collins, 1967), and of Harvey Cox, *The Secular City* (Macmillan Co., New York, 1965 and Pelican paperback, 1968). Current scientific prediction of man's future is discussed by a theologian, Hugh Montefiore, in *The Question Mark* (Collins, 1969).

Index